# THE MARK OF CAIN

# THE MARK OF CAIN:

# AN ANATOMY OF JEALOUSY

*by Marguerite and Willard Beecher*

HARPER & ROW, PUBLISHERS
New York   Evanston
1817   San Francisco   London

This book is dedicated to our teacher, the late Dr. Alfred Adler, who not only saw the danger that lurks in the use of comparisons but felt that jealous comparison was a significant subject because of its extraordinary frequency and because it disguises itself in a thousand shapes.

# CONTENTS

# PREFACE

The Epistle of James, one of the less familiar books of the New Testament to many people, makes the following categorical observation: "For where jealousy and selfish ambition exist, there will be disorder and every vile practice." (James 3:16, R.S.V.) During the past twenty years that I have been engaged in the active ministry, most of them as a hospital chaplain, I have worked with people who presented every problem that people usually bring to their ministers. These include marital problems, problems of interpersonal relations of all kinds, family problems, vocational problems, and those people who are themselves problems because they can find no satisfaction out of the ordinary business of just living. I think it is safe to say that in every one of these cases, when I have looked a little way beneath the surface, I have found these people torn with jealousy, envy, and the desire for personal prestige at the expense of others which the Epistle of James describes so tersely and so correctly. Jealousy is indeed the green-eyed monster that Shakespeare described it to be, and any clergyman who does his share of pastoral counseling will attest to the truth of this statement.

My friends Marguerite and Willard Beecher have written in the pages that follow a wise and extraordinarily lucid account of the demonic ways of jealousy and ambition. They have rightly diagnosed jealousy as a symptom of an insidious disease highly prevalent in our culture—the disease of Persisting Infantilism. Having been personal students of the great psychologist Alfred Adler, they have built upon the foundations which he laid. I know of no better statement of the meaning of jealousy and the need, therefore, to root this cancer out of our lives than you will find in this book. I am honored that I was asked by the Beechers to write this preface, and I can unhesitatingly urge all who are concerned with maturation of human beings to read and to ponder its pages.

The Rev. Alvin Van Pelt Hart

Director of Clinical Pastoral Education

St. Luke's Hospital, New York City

# THE MARK OF CAIN

# 1

## WHAT THIS IS ALL ABOUT

This is a book about jealous competition. Emotion is only a small fraction of the whole that we call jealous competition —or jealousy for short. Jealousy is a kind of over-all condition involving an individual fundamentally in his relationships with those around him. It distorts his whole perception of the world in which he is functioning. In short, the individual is more or less "out of his mind" in those areas where he is jealous.

Jealousy is usually thought of as an emotion. It is important to see that it is a comprehensive alteration of the whole way one sees and acts. When we say a person is suffering from jealousy, we must not think it is a mere discomfort of his feelings. We must see how he is caught in a bind that restricts and redirects—distorts and blackens—all that he is doing. We must see how spontaneous, happy living is impossible while he is caught in this illusion.

In this book we attempt to describe the many masks behind which jealous competition hides, and we will frequently refer to this phenomenon as jealousy, envy, rivalry, and envious or invidious comparisons. In the field of psychology, except for Alfred Adler's contributions, there has been scarcely anything written highlighting the widespread nature of this phenomenon. Even Freud paid little attention to the question of interpersonal, competitive jealousy and the manner in which it disrupts cooperation in relationships.

Generally speaking, jealousy is associated with lovers' quarrels. Other than that, most people either disclaim possession of such an emotion or are unaware that they are possessed by it. They consider it mainly—if they consider it at all—as a fault the other guy has. And yet in our observation we have found that most people, children as well as adults, are deeply affected by this emotion in varying degrees of intensity and frequency. They are largely not aware that their feeling of being second-class citizens stems from their habit of putting other people's heads higher than their own. They are given to pointing the finger of blame *outside* themselves at some other person as if that person were responsible for their discomfort and their feelings of inadequacy. No one, of course, is ever destroyed by another person in this sense. A jealous individual, or any disturbed individual, is destroyed only from *inside himself.*

In any case we concluded years ago that the habit of making jealous or invidious comparisons exists in *all* human relationships and has existed since the dawn of history not only between lovers but among siblings, in family relationships, in friendships, in the arena of sports, in the classroom, in work situations, especially in the arts and drama, and among races and nations.

Jealousy is such a significant and widespread factor in all life conflicts that much more attention should be paid to it. It is our opinion that this is the most prevalent symptom of the disease we have labeled Persisting Infantilism. We have found this disease or disability *basic to all character disorders*. We gave this label to the disease because implicit within this label lies the cure not only of the disease itself but of its multiple symptoms, especially jealous competition.

Persisting Infantilism means just what it says—continuing to act in an infantile or childish manner. People have always sensed that troublesome, burdensome individuals behave in childish ways, although mostly they have been oblivious of the obvious significance of this tendency. To act like a child means to act in a dependent, leaning, nonresponsible fashion. The cure for this disease then, with its various symptoms, would be to rehabilitate or retrain the individual until he becomes an independent, self-sufficient, responsible adult.

The mature, self-reliant, responsible individual has little or no need to make jealous comparisons—to destroy, sabotage, blackmail, exploit, lie, cheat, or otherwise torment and tear down those around him. He is too busy and concerned with building and creating and producing. His interest lies on the useful side of life. So we have found that self-reliance is the only antidote to infantile dependency.

To repeat, it is our opinion that emotional difficulties arise only in those areas in which an individual leans and depends on others rather than on his own inner voices, his own inner resources, and his own initiative. A problem is only a situation which one has not trained himself to meet in a productive way. So it seems obvious to us that the solution for an individual's emotional problems is to increase self-reliance in those areas where there has been dependency and pain. When an individual no longer leans and depends on others but brings the center of gravity back into himself, he can stand without crutches. He can "let go and walk on." Only in such circumstances, it seems to us, can a human being function as a wholly adequate person.

When we speak of self-reliance, we speak of it not only in the physical sense but also in the emotional and psychological sense, and we mean that a person must achieve non-dependence on both levels. It is our belief that all educational efforts should be directed toward starting such training as early in the life of each individual as is physically and humanly possible. Certainly we have not been and are not now producing a high enough percentage of mature, responsible adults in proportion to those who remain persistently infantile. I. A. R. Wylie said, "Many people go from infancy to senility without having achieved maturity." We concur. The fall of the Roman Empire came when the majority of Romans lost their self-reliance and depended on "slaves, bread and circuses." An infantile population harbors the seeds of its own destruction. Persisting Infantilism and atomic energy are mighty dangerous ingredients to mix together. We must either grow up or blow up!

If a disease is to be cured, its symptoms have to be recognized. The symptoms of Persisting Infantilism appear to us to be glaringly evident: passivity, aggressiveness, functional stomach disorders, headaches with no organic basis, lisping, stammering, facial distortions, negative obedience, delinquency, addiction, and *jealousy* of others. All of these are manifested in children's behavior as well as that of adults. In addition, children and infantile adults frequently have symptoms such as bed-wetting, food rejection, thumb sucking, head bumping, clicking noises in the throat, constant snapping of fingernails or knuckles, frequent crying spells, sulking, temper tantrums, and so on. All of these behaviors are indicative of Persisting Infantilism. In common parlance, they are referred to as baby tricks. But probably the most basic signifier of this disease is jealous competition or rivalry.

Parents are especially prone to overlook rivalry among siblings. Worse yet, they accept rivalry as normal behavior that will be outgrown eventually. Facts do not substantiate this. Rivalry becomes a fixed habit of mind. This symptom of jealous rivalry or competition in all human relationships is so prevalent and so disruptive of cooperation and healthy relationships that we have come to think of it as comparable to an infectious virus—an infection, as is any infection, spread by ignorance and contamination.

Because we feel so strongly about this particular symptom, we have devoted this book to it with the hope of unmasking some of its many disguises. To support our conclusions about jealous rivalry and competition, we have called in evidence any records of human experience that indicate the presence of this infection. The first record of such human experience that we present is the story of Cain and Abel in the Old Testament with our interpretation of its meaning.

There are many in this modern age who believe the Bible to be discredited. They cannot accept it on the basis of revealed religion, and no one expects them to do so. We call on it, however, because it is the crystallization of human experience from many ages. The story of Cain and Abel serves well to show that jealousy had no friends from the beginning, since it always places one at cross-purposes with others. As a matter of fact, no one in all history has spoken well of jealousy, except perhaps the person who tries to excuse himself in order to hide it from himself.

The ancients who wrote the Bible stories saw and described with cameo precision the destructive force of jealous competition in human lives. In this book our purpose will be to show again and again with what may seem to be monotonous regularity that human failures are due to the crippling effect of Persistent Infantilism—the most striking and infectious symptom of which is jealous competition.

We do not attempt to give answers or solutions or a list of formulas for the cure of jealousy in this book. We do not do this because we do not believe in how-to-do-it books. We feel that people who go around looking for formulas are not yet willing to face their problem. They want only to escape without changing their behavior.

In this book we present only the anatomy of jealousy. Or we could say that this book is like a topographical map that gives the characteristics or features of the vast territory of jealousy. We hope our readers will come to understand the nature of this trait with its many disguises and how it is used socially. Once a person fully understands something, he can invent his own way to deal with it—if he chooses to be rid of it. A famous psychiatrist, Dr. Béran Wolfe, once said: "You can't do anything to help anyone until he is willing to do anything—even get well."

## 2
## MURDERERS AND MURDEREES

There are those who no longer accept the introductory chapters of the Bible on a literal basis. Even if they are accepted as allegories, their meaning often eludes understanding. They were written in such a way that their content seems to relate only to a time long past. Few think of them as applying to the here and now. And yet they are living guides to a living present—especially the third allegory about the brothers Cain and Abel. As the story goes, all seemed to be well between these two until they started quibbling about who was better or more right. This led to murder.

We wonder if any murder, or any war for that matter, would take place if we had sense enough to hold our hot tempers until our burning pride cooled down. A small grudge and a lot of talk is like a short fuse and a keg of dynamite. Every day our newspapers report jealous feuds that started when two or more people disagreed, got into an argument, and tried to convince each other with their fists or worse, each one competing for the cheers of the onlookers. Let's take a typical report about a tavern row between an off-duty police officer and a drunk. The report states that the policeman was a plain-clothes detective who finished work about midnight and stopped at a bar to have a few drinks. He and a drunk standing at the bar got into an argument over a baseball game. Soon fists were flying until bystanders intervened. Everyone thought the trouble was over when the drunk left the bar before closing time. The detective followed fifteen minutes later. As he walked to his car fifty feet away, he was shot through the chest.

So we see that jealous competition and murder are very much with us today even as they have been from the beginning of time. The old patriarchs who wrote the Bible must have considered it a most vital matter, since they made murder, born of jealous competition, the third story in the Old Testament. They must have had a lot of experience with and understanding of human conflict. At any rate they give evidence of regarding jealousy between brothers as a real danger to the development of the individual and society.

They began their third story with clear, simple statements:

Now Adam knew Eve his wife, and she conceived and bore Cain, saying, "I have gotten a man with the help of the Lord."

And again, she bore his brother Abel. Now Abel was a keeper of sheep, and Cain a tiller of the ground.

So it has always been. People get married and have children. Their children grow up and choose some kind of occupation for themselves. They have to make a contribution to the world around them as payment for the goods and services they receive. The world survives by a division of labor. We couldn't have a world where everyone tilled the ground and no one tended sheep. We need mechanics, electricians, engineers, street cleaners, farmers, shepherds, doctors, dentists, and every imaginable contributing effort and idea. Different contributions are necessary to, and enrich, the whole community. No one basic contribution is more valuable than another in terms of survival. The best effort of each of us is needed equally. This is the reality situation as it is now and as it has always been from the beginning.

This condition had been prepared for Cain and Abel when it was said, in the first allegory, that "God created man in His Own image." Now what could the patriarchs have meant by that unless they meant that each of us was intended to be a *creator* in his own right and that this power is an inherent gift at birth? If there is a more important meaning, it has escaped us. In any case, such an interpretation helps to bring right home to us today that all of us were meant to spend our lives as inventive, ingenious, independent, and creative people.

Next, man was given a very simple instruction, "Be fruitful." And a garden was provided so that he could do just that. He was told to multiply all that was given him. What possible meaning could this have for us today? Do we each have to have a garden in order to be fruitful? Rather, doesn't it mean that each of us is supposed *to multiply and bring forth the fruits of his own ideas—each in his own way?*

Trouble seems to start only when people begin to argue about whose contribution is more important. This must have been what happened between Cain and Abel, although it isn't spelled out for us in so many words. One of them, however, must have started boasting, "What I do is better than what you do!" Haven't we all heard kids get into boasting arguments? We overheard one kid say to another, "My father can spit farther than your father can," and his playmate yelled, "Oh, no he can't! My father can spit all the way across the street." It is in just such seemingly trivial arguments that grudges are born, jealousies flourish, and fists begin to fly. Whether now or then, it means that one wants the other to take a position of permanent inferiority to himself.

Sometimes, of course, rivalries between brothers get launched because parents unwittingly show a preference. The rivalry between Cain and Abel could have started this way. Perhaps they smiled on Abel's flocks more frequently than on Cain's produce from the fields. Haven't you heard countless parents say, "Why can't you do as well as your brother?" We know a father and mother who taunted their oldest son constantly by saying, "Your brother is an angel; he was born with wings on!" It is entirely possible that rivalry started that way among the ancients, even as it does today.

But let us go on with the story of Cain and Abel as it was written:

In the course of time Cain brought to the Lord an offering of the fruit of the ground, and Abel brought of the firstlings of his flock and of their fat portions. And the Lord had regard for Abel and his offering, but for Cain and his offering he had no regard. So Cain was very angry, and his countenance fell. The Lord said to Cain, "Why are you angry, and why has your countenance fallen? If you do well, will you not be accepted? And if you do not do well, sin is couching at the door; its desire is for you, but you must master it."

Cain said to Abel his brother, "Let us go out to the field." And when they were in the field, Cain rose up against his brother Abel, and killed him.

This is the third allegory, as it was written in the Old Testament. Let us see how the same story would sound if it were reported in our daily press with modern language. It might be written as follows:

*PROMINENT FARMER KILLS RANCHER BROTHER*

Mr. Cain, well-known horticulturist and farmer, attacked and killed his brother, Mr. Abel, a wealthy ranch owner who lived next door. The two were arguing in a field when Cain picked up a rock and threw it at Abel's head, killing him.

Neighbors reported that these brothers had been rivals recently for political preferment. Each wanted to be elected "The Most Important Man" in the community. There had been a feud between them as to which had been chosen for that office. Each, in turn, claimed the victory for himself. The murder has made a run-off election unnecessary.

Mr. Cain had supplied the local markets with excellent fruits and vegetables. Mr. Abel raised the finest sheep in the state. These brothers had been known to be good friends until a popularity contest was held at the County Fair. A misunderstanding arose as to whether Cain's vegetables or Abel's sheep were to have top billing. Bystanders heard the disagreement but did not realize that they were taking the matter so seriously, since meat and vegetables were equally needed in the market place.

Apparently, the two brothers continued their argument until it led to Abel's murder. Neighbors are at a loss to understand the deeper motives for the crime. Some believe they were really fighting over government contracts and that each had been trying to make a good impression on the purchasing agent assigned by Washington to these parts.

We have purposely left out of this modern version the questions that were asked of Cain in the Old Testament version. These are very important questions because each of us, today, has to answer them every time we get trapped in a jealous competition. Now the first two questions asked of Cain, about his fallen countenance and being angry, indicate that he must have looked "green with envy." A jealous person is always an angry person. He feels put back in life. While he is in the throes of jealousy, he thinks of himself as impoverished and defrauded. Self-pity strips him of contentment. Both his past and his future seem empty to him. He is conscious only of the gnawing pain of his jealous frustration. He can't call up any successes or happiness he may have had in his past life. The story of self-pity is written on his face.

The next question was "If you do well, will you not be accepted?" Surely no more poignant question than this can be asked of any man at any time. It strips one bare and points up one's whole approach to life and to other people. Is there any other basis on which we deserve to be accepted? The person who is content to do his best trusts others to accept and to recognize the value of his contribution. He is able to live in contentment without tensions. He does not need to look to the right or to the left, and he is free to move forward without embarrassment in life. He is untroubled and serene. The success of others is no stumbling block in his path, regardless of whether they have more or less than he. Their good fortune is his good fortune, as far as he is concerned.

In the statement "If you do not do well, sin is couching at the door" there is an implication that Cain had, in some way, cheated or hadn't given the best he could give in the situation. Perhaps he hadn't brought the best fruit of the ground as his offering because he hadn't tilled the ground carefully or tended his fruits properly. He may have become so involved in watching what Abel was doing that he hadn't had sufficient time to mind his own affairs. When a person compares himself habitually with others, he spoils things for himself. He is trapped by his unfriendly comparisons. He can't coexist with his "pacemaker" without feeling put back in his own eyes. Lacking a way to cut him down to size, he builds up tensions that wreck his own health and happiness. In the end he often prefers to destroy his opposition—as Cain did.

We are not told what happened in the field before Cain

killed Abel. We are left to wonder if something was finally said that triggered Cain's envy to the point where he could no longer stand the pain of it. Did Abel brag in a loud-mouthed way? Did he lord it over his brother? We shall never know what it was that made Cain feel there was no recourse but murder.

A friend of ours once said, "The world is full of just two kinds of people—murderers and murderees." He liked to furnish proof that the murdered one often invites murder. Of course it is our tradition to give all our sympathy to the one who gets murdered. But isn't it possible that we might spread our sympathy around if we knew all the circumstances in each situation of this type? Might we not find that many of the Abels of the world invite stoning by the Cains? Was there ever a tug of war with only one man pulling on the rope? Could there be a struggle for dominance or a stalemate in any situation unless two or more toiled in opposition to each other?

If Cain had listened to the Lord's words he might have redeemed himself, for it is written, according to the allegory, that the Lord said, "Its desire is for you, but you must master it." This means that the man who has "fallen" into jealous competition can find his way back if he chooses. He can be redeemed or restored if he rids himself of wasting his time in jealous comparisons and goes back to his *original state of being the creator he was created to be.* But as long as he retains his jealous habit of mind it makes no difference whether he has scarcity or abundance—he remains at war with himself and others. As did Cain.

After the killing, Cain was called to a reckoning:

The Lord said to Cain, "Where is Abel your brother?" He said, "I do not know; am I my brother's keeper?"

But the Lord told him that his brother's blood cried out from the ground and that when he tilled the ground (in jealous competition) it would not henceforth yield unto him its strength. And this curse was placed on Cain and all who have come after him and been so afflicted:

"You shall be a fugitive and a wanderer on the earth."

3

## AN APPROACH TO JEALOUSY

We were first alerted to the psychological implications of jealous comparisons by our teacher, the late Dr. Alfred Adler, the famous Viennese psychologist and founder of Individual Psychology. To show the universality of human behavior in all ages, Adler often used anecdotes and quoted from Bible stories, poets, playwrights, philosophers, and other sources. His teaching brought fresh insight to us about the danger that lurks in the use of jealous comparison.

Early in our work as Individual Psychologists, we began to observe and to become aware of the extent to which jealous comparison permeated every area of human relationships though it disguised itself in a thousand shapes. For more than a score of years, our work in parent-child guidance, adult counseling, group discussions, personnel work, teaching, and lecturing has involved us with human beings spanning the ages from childhood to the golden years. No matter what the age of those with whom we have worked, our findings have been the same in respect to this problem. That is, we have found ourselves primarily and almost continuously confronted with the need of devising techniques for helping adults as well as children to understand and to deal with or resolve such personal problems as feeling put down, measuring oneself as less than or getting less than someone else, viewing another pasture as greener than one's own, keeping a rosary of grudges about being less favored or less loved than another, and struggling to be one up on or to surpass another.

The techniques we have devised for meeting such problems have their basis in one of the tenets of Individual Psychology. Adler said, "All problems are social problems in a social setting and there are no other problems." This means that no human problem is, in reality, a one-ness thing but always a two-or-more-ness thing. We have been mindful of this in all of our work whether we were dealing with groups of individuals or with a single individual, seven or forty-seven or more years old. And so, we have found it effective (1) to confront the child or the adult with his jealous and resultant unfriendly way of looking at others and relating to them, (2) to reveal to him how his jealous comparisons have tripped him up by diverting or destroying his energies away from his own initiative and creativity, (3) to point out how this has increased his dependency on the opinion and the help of others, kept him infantile, and prevented his making the helpful contribution society expects of him, and (4) to challenge him to move in more friendly, cooperative, mature, and constructive directions in life.

This type of approach seems to us to be singularly important when dealing with children. We believe that the most significant transactions any educator can have with a child are those that help him to gain the courage to trust himself so that he will not feel he must protect his life against his fellow man by jealous competition. The goal of the jealous person is to be the preferred and only one. Society grants no one this exclusive privilege. Therefore, it is our opinion that the most vital task a parent or any educator has is to present the picture of the outside world to a child in such a way that he finds joy in letting go of his infantile demand for such special privilege so that he may join the common activities of daily life as a participating member and so that adulthood will not be a stranger to him. Every child should be helped to understand the fundamental design of man in society and the demands society inevitably makes upon all of its members. Only with such an apperceptive scheme will a child develop fellow feeling and social interest. It was Adler's opinion that all failures in life are failures because they are lacking in fellow feeling and social interest; that the meaning they give to life is a private meaning; and that no one else benefits by the achievement of their aims and that their interest stops short of their own persons.

Let us take a closer look at the frame of reference within which Individual Psychologists work. The Individual Psychologist engages in a mutual inquiry or dialogue with the individual who comes for help and shows a genuine interest by attempting to see with the other person's eyes and listen with his ears. In so doing, his aim is (1) to discover the goal and the guiding or fictive image around which the whole life style of the individual is developed or organized—his design for living which grows out of his goal; and (2) to determine the individual's mistaken attitudes which are also inherent in his goal and the misconceptions about reality which are the basis of his discomfort or unhappiness. With such an understanding, the Individual Psychologist can see and show the individual that what has occurred did not necessarily have to occur—that it is only one of the possible choices or ways of relating that could happen. Also, if we can go so far as to see that, given the same mistaken picture of the world of reality and the same erroneous goal, we would probably have done likewise, then we lose any inclination to sit in judgment or to condemn. But, even more important, we are able to see that the whole personality is a unity which shows the same direction of movement at whatever point it is observed—that all the aspects of the individual's behavior are directed toward attaining his particular goal.

Adler once said: "The most important question is not whence? but whither? Only when we know the active, directive goal of a person may we undertake to understand his movements." This statement is important because it stresses that behavior is purposive and does not have to be explained in terms of a cause reaching out of the past, driving one to do what he does. In other words, it is not necessary to know or to search in the past of an individual to change his behavior. Moreover, this statement indicates the importance of the movements or relationships an individual makes. Adler used to say to us: "Watch only movement. What a person does is what a person means." By this he meant that we may arrive at the meaning a person has given to life if we simply watch what he does in life—which way his feet are going. If his feet and his mouth aren't together, which shall we trust? If a person says: "I don't have a jealous bone in my body," but everything the person does shows his jealous, envious striving to be ahead of others, what shall we believe, his feet or his mouth?

So our work is fundamentally with the relationships a person is making in the here-and-now when confronted by problems of the outside world. He doesn't relate himself in some predetermined manner. He relates himself according to his own interpretation of himself and his present situation. He sees all his personal problems from a perspective that is his own creation—his own style of life. A mistaken direction, as a result of a mistaken view of life, always reveals itself clearly in asocial behavior.

Adler felt that anyone's life style was formulated and established by five years of age, and that, because of his inexperience and lack of judgment, the child will, of course, make wrong assumptions of what the world of reality is all about; and he felt that a mistaken interpretation of life could be altered only by the individual's (either child or adult) own recognition of the faults and errors in his early judgment about life. He was fond of saying that "man knows more than he understands," and so he had great confidence in the individual's ability, once given insight, to understand and to accept the truth about the reality situation of the outside world. He used to maintain that he had never found anyone to whom it would not have been possible to explain his erroneous mechanism. And he felt that for an individual to realize a mistake and its bad consequences and not try to amend it was contrary to human nature and against the principle of self-preservation.

Adler harbored this opinion because he believed that, with a *persistent,* mistaken law-of-motion, a person (1) would run counter to the idea of cooperation and that he would come into contradiction with social feeling and the relentless demands of the ideal community of mankind, and (2) he would feel the manifold consequences of this collision. Were it not for the relentless demands of community living, everyone could, in the course of his life, satisfy his wrong law-of-motion. But Adler was confident that the individual, in so doing, would bow more or less willingly to the iron law of community living. Only a child or an adult pampered and spoiled to the utmost would expect and demand to make use of the contributions of the community for himself without contributing fully in return.

So the question that Cain asked of the Lord: "Am I my brother's keeper?" really springs from the inseparable connectedness of mankind and arises out of the stern criterion of the ideal community. Adler, therefore, conceived the proposition that "only he who carries within himself, in his law-of-movement, a sufficient degree of the community ideal and lives according to it as easily as he breathes, will be in a position to solve, in the meaning of community, those conflicts which are inevitably his."

The pampered child or adult, not trained for self-reliance and contribution, is in a difficult position. He finds himself defective in ways that prevent his being useful. Any symptoms he develops, as a result, are merely his inadequate, futile attempts to solve his problems by the device of making the kind of trouble that brings others to his aid. In other words, he exploits those around him to make up for his own inadequacy. Therefore, his emotional and psychological difficulties arise because he leans on and depends on others.

The one who uses others as his crutch lacks the courage and training to stand on his own two feet. If no effort is made to increase his courage and to train him to be self-reliant, he begins eventually to make jealous comparisons between himself and others his age who are moving forward in life. This leads to his developing multiple feelings of inferiority. If he isn't trained to act more courageously and independently, his feelings of inferiority will accumulate and become a lasting undercurrent in his life. Accumulated feelings of inferiority result in leading the individual to make a compensating movement toward feelings of superiority, which are a way of seeking power to control and to dominate. These feelings of superiority will become equal, though opposite, to his feelings of inferiority and they will be in direct conflict to any demands for cooperation. That is, his feelings of superiority will put him on the useless side of life because his real problem of leaning and depending on others is not being solved. These superiority feelings will manifest themselves in many ways—in pride, in boasting, in vain ambitions, in personal aggrandizement, in depreciation of others and a jealous struggle to be dominant in order to maintain the special privilege to which he has become accustomed.

This type of behavior always puts the pampered, dependent, leaning individual at cross-purposes to those in his environment who, in time, will experience him as a disturbing element. His way of relating not only will bring him into conflict with others in his environment but will place him in contact with the dark side of life and prevent him from finding any joy in living. He will be neither a happy nor a free soul capable of developing his own inborn potentialities and his own spontaneity, which is his birthright, for he will always be caught in conflict between his demand for special privilege and the demands for cooperation on the part of those around him. In subsequent chapters of this book, we will develop this theme again and again.

To repeat, the solution to such an individual's problem is to increase his courage to face the reality situation confronting him and to train him to be self-reliant in those areas where he has formerly leaned on, depended on, and exploited others to do for him what he should rightly always have done for himself. Nature expects each creature to develop and maintain his own initiative, which means to become personally responsible in life—to keep one's own show on the road.

In the light of all this, let us consider Andrea, an eight-year-old girl who was caught in a jealous struggle to maintain her dominant position in the family. When she was brought to us for help, all her family and her school were experiencing her as a most disturbing element. But first we must explain how we, personally, incorporate the concepts of Individual Psychology in our way of operating in any case of parent-child guidance.

We treat total family relationships rather than only the offending member because we know no child exists in a vacuum but is a part of the social fabric of the whole family. We view a family as we would a jigsaw puzzle that fits into one frame; to change one piece, all the others must be changed correspondingly. We know that many patient sheep can lie down in one stall, but one unfair, restless sheep starts all trampling each other. Once trampling has started, it is necessary to deal with all simultaneously.

One of us works with the so-called problem child for the first forty minutes of the appointment hour in one room while the other works, in another room, with the parents, siblings, or any other family member who is involved. During this time, it has been our experience that each complains about the other; the child complains about the family and the family complains about the child and about each other's handling of the child. No one blames himself for anything. Each acts like God's special agent put on earth to criticize others. Each has a private blueprint of how things should go.

The last twenty minutes of the appointment we come together in one room for what we call a Joint Conference. With all present, each is challenged to be personally responsible for his own behavior instead of trying to be Moses and to write the Ten Commandments for others. In other words, we work together to build a family Master Plan that guarantees fair play for all members. Families come to us deadlocked in mutual resentment. So in the very first conference, we begin to disrupt the whole family situation because we have learned that nothing constructive will grow while all the members of the family are locked in the struggle of their old competitive jealousy and mutual sabotage. By showing all the members of the family the total picture, we thereby put each member on record in what might be called a goldfish bowl. Thereafter, each member has to watch his own behavior. If he does not, he is quickly brought into line by the other members of the family each time he reverts to his old exploitative behavior. Each member, then, holds the others to the new family plan—a Magna Carta, structured for mutual advantage instead of special privilege.

In restructuring family relationships, we have found that neither the parents nor the child are aware of the over-all basic mistakes they make. They do not interpret their old familiar patterns as mistakes. Our role is to expose these to both the parents and the child, and most especially to expose the mistaken subsidies that are keeping the child infantile so that he falls behind other children who are learning to be more independent.

In working with the child alone, no matter what his age, he is treated as a responsible person in his own right and not as something precious out of Peter Pan. There is a frank discussion about those things he is doing that are not helpful or useful and how they damage those around him. The child's intelligence is never underestimated, and so there is no talking down to him. As Adlerians, we are not so much concerned with the child's emotions as with the *uses* he makes of them, especially the unfair uses to gain his own jealous and selfish ends within the family.

It is assumed that the child cannot "see the forest for the

trees"; so, as the discussions with him progress, each tree is labeled for what it is. It is explained to him that we are starting an investigation together which will concern itself with the search for clues as to why he is dissatisfied, discouraged, or unhappy. And in each discussion, an attempt is made to undermine the child's persisting, infantile dependence and to prepare him to reorient himself toward a more grown-up goal in life than the one he has been using. At the same time, he is given a point of reference for appraising human behavior in general and specifically furnishing him a way to estimate for himself the degree of his own mistaken manner of perceiving and behaving.

Since every stick has two ends, we know that it is a rare child indeed who will make use of this new behavior-yardstick until or unless the adults in his environment are willing concurrently to alter their inadequate behavior. Some astute wit said, "Children are natural mimics; they act just like their parents despite every effort to teach them good manners!" We have found that when and if a child's parents mend their own bad manners and begin to operate on a more common-sense, realistic basis, the discussions that have been held with the child take on significant meaning and make it less possible or urgent for him to continue in his old, jealous, mistaken direction with any kind of a clear conscience.

Andrea's case illustrates how we work with a child and what a first Joint Conference is like. All we knew about Andrea, previous to her family bringing her to us, was that she was eight and that the school was coming to the conclusion that she was "mentally retarded."

The first day she was brought for help, we concluded on the basis of her responses and the manner in which she conducted herself that Andrea was not retarded but only an excessively spoiled, pampered, and dependent child. We saw her as an intelligent little trickster who used the pretense or appearance of helplessness so that she might live, as Adler would say, "as a worm in an apple." Our observation was verified when we found out how Andrea habitually behaved at home. We learned that she would, for example, purposely button her clothes up wrong to attract attention and get some member of the family to rebutton them. She would leave all the food on her plate untouched until everyone at the table had begged her to eat it. She frowned continuously as if she were a queen whose disfavor had been deliberately courted by all the members of the family. She used fear of thunder or the doctor or anything else she could dream up as an excuse for a big deal. Each member of the family waited on Andrea hand and foot. In addition to other services, her parents did her schoolwork for her. The grandmother, who lived in the home, anticipated her every wish. A brother and sister, several years her senior, waited on and pampered her, too.

In short, the whole household pivoted around Andrea. They had been doing this since she was born; at that time, their living quarters had been small and cramped. So they had dressed Andrea in frilly doll-like clothes and sat her on a satin pillow on the couch in their small living room. She looked like a doll, acted like one, and was treated like one. By the time she was four, her pediatrician had labeled her "mentally retarded."

Now that she was eight, the whole household was experiencing her as a most disturbing element, and Andrea was caught in a jealous struggle to maintain her dominant position —that of being the most loved and the most favored. No wonder her performance record was low in school, where no one can hope to have such a dominant position. In any case, daily frustration and hostility had become the hallmark of the home. The older brother and sister had become locked in a jealous competition to grab off whatever little attention they could attract by trying on their own to out-baby their baby sister. It was, in reality, a three-way, jealous competition among all these children to see which could get the biggest slice of attention.

During the forty-minute period of the first interview with Andrea, she frowned and pretended not to understand what it was all about. These emotional efforts of hers were ignored and she was treated with solemnity as if she were Senator Margaret Chase Smith! Explanations were made to reveal to Andrea her jealous struggle to be the most loved and the most favored, the tricks she used to hold the center of attention and get others to do things for her that she should, at eight, be doing for herself.

In the Joint Conference that followed, the last twenty minutes of the hour, it was explained to all—parents, grandmother, brother, and sister—in Andrea's hearing that they lived with a very intelligent little girl who had trapped them all into doing her bidding by using apparent helplessness, appearing not to understand and frowning as if she were a queen and they were all her disloyal subjects. They were told that Andrea had put the whammy on them all and forced them to be her captive audience. They were informed that they had to learn how to be more clever and how to outfox Andrea so that they could escape the traps that Andrea set for them. At this point, everyone laughed in recognition of the situation, including Andrea.

Mother and father were asked not to do Andrea's homework for her, because this was her responsibility, not theirs, and they were asked not to beg her to eat but simply remove her plate at meal's end, even if she hadn't taken a bite. They were also informed that if Andrea wanted to button her clothes all wrong, they should be gracious enough to allow her this privilege and to wear dark glasses so they would not see her frowns. Grandmother was urged to look the other way and run to the nearest exit so she would no longer be tempted to play the role of Andrea's mind reader. Brother and sister were instructed to mend their own fences, which should keep them so busy they wouldn't have time to fix things up for Andrea. All were assured that, if they did these things, Andrea would move full steam ahead because no actress plays to an empty house. And Andrea? She was challenged to learn to be a help and not a burden.

This is a sample of the way we disrupt the mistaken equilibrium of a family locked in jealous competition during a first Joint Conference and is typical of all other subsequent conferences when we check off the jealous dependency problems that are presented as they arise and are solved.

The definitive changes in Andrea's family and in her, as well as in other families who have come to us for help, have been for us a testimony to Adler's belief that "man knows more than he understands," and to his confidence in any individual's ability, once given insight, to understand and accept the truth of any reality situation.

## 4

## *MARTYR BY CHOICE*

One should look with deep suspicion on those who play the role of martyr. Their self-sacrifice is really a cloak to hide their ambition for personal recognition—their desire to win praise above others. They suffer from halo pressure; they are boastful.

In this sense we are mindful of Mr. B., a typical martyr by choice, who was jealous of his three brothers. He claimed that they had more fun than he ever had because he was a serious child. Now that his brothers work with him in their deceased father's business, he makes them pay for having a better time than he did. He punishes them by using his disability (martyrdom) as a virtue in order to belittle them. But he still has no joy in his work for his brothers are still happy sinners while he is the sad-eyed saint. Even his weekends upset him because he has to contend with his wife and his mother-in-law.

It is interesting to see how completely we expose our habit of jealous competition when we are least aware of what we are saying about ourselves. It blows through the following conversation of this troubled man like a prevailing wind. For us the direction of the wind was unmistakable. Our running commentary will so indicate. Listen to Mr. B.

I am always tired but can't relax. I try to relax but get gloomy when I do. I am run down and have low blood pressure. My doctor says I am too conscientious. I try to do too much each day. On weekends I am always worse because I must be careful how I talk to my wife and mother-in-law.

This is the way Mr. B. began. Right off he sets the stage for us. We may guess that we are about to hear a Greek tragedy in which one mortal man will contend against implacable Fates who conspire to block him. He is the "Good One." His doctor thinks so too. Certainly one could not lift a hand against someone whose only weakness is to be "too conscientious." No wonder he is tired! Only a hero would undertake such labors. Why is he not appreciated properly? Jealous competition lies in wait, of course. His wife and his mother-in-law are there to trip him on weekends and he must "be careful." They are enemies against whom he must contend. He obviously must regard them as stronger since he feels he must guard his tongue. We can only wonder what punishments would lie in store if his tongue slipped and he told them what he really thought.

I am always tense. I find fault with the performance of other people and know that I can do better than they do.

Well, no sooner is the curtain up on our drama than we find him jousting like a knight in armor. He takes on all comers and is certain he can do better in the situation than they do.

Just think of the number of unfriendly comparisons he must make each day to be sure he is superior to all of them! That must be exhausting work in itself. When does he find time to do his job? He has to watch everyone all the time and find fault. He has to be a wise man to separate so little good from so much evil all day long. We wonder what other labors he performs.

The situation got worse three years ago.

Now, we must be prepared to see some new actors arrive on the stage. They must be especially powerful enemies who threaten him.

My three brothers, my parents and I all lived under the same roof. My brothers and I work in my father's business. Then my parents died. The responsibility for everything and everyone fell on me. I am the "brains." One of my brothers is the "back" of the business.

So, now we see it! Which is more important in the sight of the Lord—the brain or the back of a body? Here again are Cain and Abel! With them the argument had been sheep versus field crops. In this instance, we have brain versus back. And, as in all such useless arguments, we know that someone is going to be hurt. We do not have to wait long to find out which one screams in pain the sooner. It is revealed in Mr. B.'s next statement.

I was always a serious child and never learned to play. I did not mingle with others because I do not like everybody.

Well, none of us likes everybody, but we usually find a few with whom we can enjoy life—that is, unless we are as competitive as Mr. B. seems to be. Looking for the faults of others as he does, we can be sure he will find no one to admire and enjoy. It is only when we feel equal to people that we can play with them. No one can avoid feelings of tension if he feels those around him are either "above" or "below" him in value. Such a one has the Mark of Cain and is doomed to roam the world alone as long as he retains the mark on his brow.

There is much detail in our business and it requires constant attention. However, we do not make much money. I am the only one who looks ahead. My brothers just go along. They are not ambitious.

Well, now, what does he expect of a "back" except that it must always go along with the "brain"? He strives to be the center of operations in the business. His brothers are willing to let him be what he wishes. If they tried to challenge him, he would be angry about that, they must have discovered. At least there is an implication here that Mr. B. can gain eminence only as things stand.

My ambition is to build a good business and to have all of us brothers stick together.

Does this mean that the "brain" is just as dependent on the "back" as the "back" is on the "brain"? Why does he contend with such stupid, lazy loafers? Why can't the brain go in business for himself and hire others to work for him? What is this mysterious attraction that leads Mr. B. to hang onto these incompetents? Again we do not have long to wait before he answers these questions.

I am so exhausted that I have got over wanting bigger things. I can't let go during the day, thinking of what must be done tomorrow. I feel I must carry the burden through. I just don't trust my brothers. I tell others what to do. If they fail, I gloat over them. I hold post-mortems over their mistakes.

Now we understand the point at which Cain picked up the rock and threw it at Abel! Mr. B. gloats over his fallen enemies —his brothers. Post-mortems over the mistakes of others are always a way of rubbing the salt of one's personal superiority into their already smarting flesh. None of us enjoys being placed in the position of permanent inferiority!

I set up new ideas and submit them to my brothers. They always disagree—but I finally have my own way about things.

Mr. B. enjoys tormenting his brothers, we see. If he were told that he is sadistic, he couldn't believe it. But what he does is like baiting bears in a pit from which they cannot escape. Mr. B. knows in advance that his brothers will do as he says in the final analysis. However, he seems to enjoy going through the pretense of giving them a choice—only to snatch it back as soon as they reach for it! He wants a setup where the other fellow has no choice, not an honest fight.

I had a hard start in life. I like to see football games but I can never find the time. I wanted to make this business succeed for my brothers' sake so that they would have a better time in life than I had. I do not check on their every move but I know that they never look ahead.

Isn't what he is saying here that he might have time for some fun if his brothers had a brain in their heads? He doesn't check every move they make, he says. Maybe not, but he waits until they take enough rope so that he can hang them for their stupidity, doesn't he? If he were to check each step they took, wouldn't their mistakes be his own? It serves his purpose better this way. He can degrade them with their own cooperation!

I set up the business giving them an equal share with me. Getting all that done has taken its toll on me. In the beginning I felt good, but now I don't.

Now we are reminded of the punishment meted out to Cain. God said to him: "When thou tillest the ground, it shall not yield unto thee her strength; a fugitive and a vagabond shalt thou be in the earth." Mr. B. has no satisfaction from his good deeds—no matter what his toil and sacrifice—since he is caught in jealous competition.

Once I decided that it was time for my brothers to take some responsibility and to speak up. I thought they should furnish some of the ideas for the future. But they never came forward with anything. I am progressive. My brothers think of everything in a different light. It is only long afterwards that they come to agree with me. Now I just let things slide until they come to see things my way. Every now and then, I walk out on them—but I always return for more punishment.

From this it is apparent that Mr. B. now uses stronger weapons in the fight against his brothers. He has found how effective the weapon of passive sabotage is. He walks out on his brothers. Since they have always allowed him to be the "brain," they take him back each time, only to have the fight renewed. For the moment, the price of his return is their complete submission. Then it all builds up into the same old deadlock.

My wife and I do not associate with my brothers socially. We do not like their friends and what they do. We avoid them. We know, of course, that they talk about us behind our backs.

What else could we expect but this? We cannot imagine that Mr. B. would confine his jealous competition only to business affairs. A virus is a virus. It accompanies us wherever we go. So, we find that Mr. B. sits in judgment on his brothers' social life just as he belittles them in the office. We do not wonder that he feels alone and broods since he can find no one at any time, in any place, who is worthy of his companionship!

There was more in Mr. B.'s conversation but it was an

unending repetition of the same theme. There is no need to record it. What we have recorded reveals his "stream of consciousness," which is only another way of saying that his conversation reveals the prevailing wind of his outlook toward life. Need we wonder why he can't relax or why he always feels tired and gloomy? Since he has eyes and ears only for slights and insults, he finds them in everything that happens. He seeks only to find fault with others. That is not difficult for anyone to find if that is all one looks for in his fellow man. Mr. B. is wholly alienated from himself!

The jealous person truly "wanders as a vagabond in a foreign land." If we mind the other fellow's business instead of our own, we have indeed abandoned our own native land to wander on foreign soil where we are not citizens. As vagabonds we must obey the law of the alien land and not find a rest for our heads.

Psychiatrists are sometimes called "alienists." How apt this designation is! Most of the cases they must treat are not organically based. Most of them are concerned with people who are alienated from themselves—who, in other words, are minding other people's business in jealous competition.

Thus do we betray ourselves in what we say and do. The mark of Cain cannot be hidden!

# 5

## *MATURITY AND IMMATURITY*

Most of us have been so contaminated by jealous competition all our lives that we do not know what mental health would be like in ourselves or in others. Our tendency is to justify our jealous strivings and our nervous tensions by pointing to the condition of our friends who suffer as much as we do from the same complaint. We argue that this is the normal state of man.

Every once in a while, however, we run into a person who makes us wonder about ourselves and distrust our own arguments on this score. We notice that he seems able to mind his own business and not meddle in the lives of those around him. We begin to look at him with awe. We wonder why he isn't the nervous type like us. How can he stand noise, confusion, and similar petty discomforts without going to pieces as we do? And just why doesn't he have to own all the latest gadgets, the most expensive things, the largest house in town, to be content? How can he discuss politics, religion, race relations, and other controversial subjects without becoming either offensive or defensive about them? How does he manage to meet good fortune without getting puffed up and bragging to all his neighbors? Or how does he endure disappointments and the frustration of his hopes without losing courage and giving up the fight? Why is he so different from others?

All these achievements, of course, are signs of the mature individual. Such people are so scarce as to be almost unforgettable when we meet them. In their presence we are sharply aware of the trivial things to which we habitually react like children. The genuinely mature individual seems to function like a well-oiled machine. Most of us pop off like a penny string of firecrackers most of the time. If we are praised we puff up out of shape. If someone finds fault with us we are deflated, crushed, ashamed to show our face.

In the presence of mature persons we realize that we are "not ourselves" most of the time. By comparison we exercise very little control of our lives and our own behavior. What is it that gets into us that reduces us to ridiculous, childish behavior? Is there a chance that we might learn to behave like grownups?

The mature individual seems to have overcome the habit of jealous competition to a large degree. His source of power or center of gravity lies within himself. He doesn't have to lean or depend on others for his inspiration, support, direction, or approval. He doesn't have to live by the customs and judgments of the crowd. He is sufficiently secure to make his own decisions as to what is right or wrong for him. He remains an inner-directed person in the face of all temptation or babble of voices in the crowd.

This seems to be the natural state of man when he is not poisoned with the virus of jealous competition. The virus apparently doesn't infect a person unless he has larceny in his heart. The dictionary defines jealousy as "fear and resentment toward a rival," and competition is defined as "the act of trying to gain something sought by another." According to these two definitions, the virus would seem to be an explosive mixture of hate, fear, and larceny.

To understand exactly how this virus can end in crippling, we must understand how it undermines a personality. We need to have a picture in our minds of how it starts and how it progresses until an individual loses his own identity and becomes depersonalized until he is like a puppet manipulated by outside forces. A little drama will serve to show the process of deterioration.

The curtain rises. The cast of characters are you and your neighbor, Charles. The two of you have been close friends for years. Both of you have about the same advantages as all the others in the neighborhood. Then one day you inherit some money. About the same time you get your name in the paper for your ideas on civic improvement. The mayor and other dignitaries call on you. Little by little you have to give more and more time to the new duties and responsibilities heaped upon you. Charles sees less and less of you because you are seldom around the house or neighborhood any more.

He begins to concentrate with a singleness of purpose on everything that happens to you—your growing prestige, your new friends, the new car and furniture you've bought and the remodeling and enlarging of your house. Then he finds himself looking out from behind his curtains to see who comes and goes at your house. He sees you the night you stagger home drunk at two in the morning and wonders where and with whom you've been celebrating. He watches where you go one day after work and makes note of the strange, attractive woman with you in an out-of-the-way cocktail lounge.

He picks up and repeats the gossip that you are living beyond your means in spite of that big inheritance. He is convinced you don't like to be with poorer friends like him any more. Those excuses and smiles you keep giving him no longer fool him. He was good enough company for you before you got to going around with big shots, but not any more. He can remember when your wife wore cloth coats instead of mink, as his wife is still having to do. No, it isn't jealousy, he assures himself. Some people just get more than they deserve in the world, and while the "hogs get fatter," the rest of us have to do without! He dreams about the day you will be broke at the rate you are going through your money. Then he visualizes how you will come hanging around him again. You will probably want to borrow money from him. Then who will be the big shot?

Now what has been going on in this drama? What really happened to friend and neighbor Charles? If we break it down we find:

1. He stopped minding his own business.

2. He began to keep his eyes on you and on your business.

3. In his eyes you grew taller, more powerful and masterful.

4. You had him hypnotized so he could no longer see anything or think of anything or do anything but keep watching you.

5. He spent his time sitting up nights until you came home, to see what you were doing. He lost touch with his former self. His jealousy led him to feel like a nonentity.

6. His own home, his own life, and all that had had meaning for him turned to ashes; there no longer seemed to be

anything interesting or nourishing in his life; he had lost his own way of life but couldn't go your way; he began to hate himself and you.

This is but a fragment of what happens in attacks of jealousy. It establishes the key, however, to all such situations. The one constant factor is the loss of personal identity through abdication to outside influence or control.

What Charles did in this situation makes clear how it is that anyone loses his birthright as a first-class citizen. Feelings of inferiority continue until one no longer makes comparisons between his own activities and those of another person. As long as Charles places his neighbor's head higher than his own he is caught in a race against him since he cannot endure the feeling of inferiority he creates out of his picture projection.

In a race of this type the rival is paced by the person in the lead, and he feels obliged to overtake the leader in the competition. In other words, Charles is in a hypnotic bind and the neighbor is his pacemaker. He loses his initiative to his neighbor, who seems to control him. This is why any jealous person appears to others to be under the control of the one he envies and pursues.

Nothing can liberate the envious person until he sees that he is the source of his own painful situation. Until he can see and accept this, he will not be free of the hell he creates emotionally by making invidious comparisons. A person grows according to his own inner nature or innate genius when his view is not distorted by jealousy. When one lets go of comparisons he is restored to his own initiative and is free to discover the path ahead for himself.

Maturity is serenity, and serenity is the natural state of the mind when it is free of jealousy. It is comparable to the "Peace that passeth all understanding." It is as a millpond at twilight that mirrors the geese as they fly overhead but does not hold their image when they have passed. Free of all seeking or grasping and the tensions of jealous desire, maturity is the serenity of the millpond when it is no longer torn by the passing wind.

# 6
## UNFAIR COMPETITION

Seven-year-old Jimmy was already an alien in his native land. He was completely out of control both at home and at school. It was not safe to leave him unattended when other children were around because of his cruelty. He pulled chairs out from under them when they were not looking; he pushed them downstairs; he aimed bricks at their heads in the playground; he smashed up bottles and tried to throw broken glass in their eyes. He stole and talked of nothing but blood and murder. He dreamed about witches and poisons.

We are reminded, when we speak of Jimmy, of what the Lord said in his heart, after many generations of Adam:

The Lord saw that the wickedness of man was great in the earth, and that every imagination of the thoughts of his heart was only evil continually. (Genesis 6:5 R.S.V.)

The Lord did not say that children were born that way. Nor was Jimmy. He was the first-born son of well-educated, upper-middle-class parents. He lived with them in a good section of the city in a comfortable and attractive home. His father worked for a large corporation. His mother owned and was the headmistress of a private school. With such a situation, why was Jimmy racing pell-mell down the path of hatred? Why didn't he feel at home in his native land?

Perhaps there was no welcome mat out when he arrived. His mother had wanted a girl baby. She feared men. She could remember only one thing about her father. "All he did was spank us," she said. There was a certain unfriendliness in her manner—a coldness and hardness. When this boy came, her fundamental feelings were not those of affection or acceptance.

Jimmy was never abused or neglected. Quite the contrary. His physical well-being became a matter of constant attention. Early in his life he had a series of earaches and abscesses which temporarily interfered with his hearing and required much treatment by ear specialists. When his teeth came in, they were widely spaced at first. His mother felt his teeth were ugly and was critical both of the way his teeth looked and the way he spoke, although there was no marked deformity or any evidence of a speech defect. His mother's unfriendly comments, however, led Jimmy to become self-conscious and hesitant in his early talking days, and, gradually, he learned to use speech as a weapon of attack. Thus for the first five years of his life, in addition to his parents, there were doctors, dentists, and ear and speech specialists concerning themselves with the child's physical well-being.

No, Jimmy was not neglected, but he was, just the same, in a very dangerous situation. Like any first child in a family, while he remains the only child, Jimmy developed a false picture of life. The only child's parents are apt to be overconscientious, overconcerned, and oversolicitous. In this respect Jimmy's mother outdid herself even though she would much rather have had a girl baby. We might say then that Jimmy occupied the position of a person who has lived for many years on an unusually large income that he has inherited and has been able to spend without counting the outlay. If a depression comes along, a large part of one's capital is removed and the pennies have to be counted. The penury of such a situation is bitterly felt. Jimmy was to have a similar experience. For five years, he had been wealthy in terms of attention. He had come to take it for granted and to view it as a kind of base pay for being alive. It seemed little enough to him and he measured any gains from that point upward. He had not had to share his wealth with anyone. He had no preparation for any deprivation or depression.

After five years, Jimmy experienced a full-fledged depression in the form of a baby sister. The depression that hit him, however, was more extreme than most first-born children experience. His sister, Debbie, was delivered at five and a half months, and lived. News of this "miracle baby" spread. Doctors and newspaper men flocked to the house to observe her and to ask questions. There were many newspaper stories and articles written about her. In all the furor, Jimmy was completely overlooked.

Worse yet, he was due to begin school just at this time. This was double jeopardy. He had had no preparation for give and take. He had no idea that he was to be one of twenty or thirty other children who would expect and demand to share the attention of one teacher. He would resist such an experience even if he weren't leaving a bundle of competition at home. Should we be surprised that he bitterly resented the demands of the situation? How could anyone expect him to attack bravely through the front door to the outside world when such a formidable enemy was storming the rear gate at home? How could he pay attention to what was going on at school or be expected to like anything about it?

Going to school was bad enough, but Jimmy was to realize more fully the extent of his plight as time went on. It was bad enough, when he got home from school, to witness the look of adoration in his mother's eyes when she gazed on this baby girl she had always wanted. What he couldn't understand was why his father, too, surfeited her with so much attention and affection. He had no way of understanding about her delicate delivery or that her life had hung in the balance. As far as he was concerned she was just a greedy little monster—she got so much more than he had ever had. He hated her already.

He was soon to learn to hate her more when she began to walk and talk. There were many occasions that compounded his hatred. The toy top experience for one. He was just trying to master the trick of spinning the new top he had been given when Debbie hove in sight. She began dancing around him and yelling, "Let me see it—let me have it—let me play with it!" Mother was never long moving into action at times like this. He did not have to wait long this time before she appeared on the scene and said, "Give your little sister the top." That does it. Who could ever possibly want a little sister at any such price? Nothing he has is really his—ever. Debbie can get anything if she yells loud enough. She is never made to think of his rights and his possessions. And so the gulf between them was widened by that much.

So Jimmy has to let her play with his top. What else is there for him to do but retire in sullen, jealous anger and bide his time? He begins to consider how to get even and get his top back. His mother shortly disappears in the kitchen. Now is the time. He grabs his top and gives Debbie a whack. At first, she's taken aback with surprise. She's never at a loss, though. She has always figured that he was expendable, and she has always found some way to deal with him. So, she lets go with hysterical, uncontrolled, anguished screams.

Mother comes flying in from the kitchen trembling with alarm. With dots and dashes of Morse-code shrieks and sobs, Debbie enlarges on the attack made on her. Jimmy gets no chance to explain that all he wanted was to get back his own top from her. His mother flies at him in rage. "How dare you hit your little sister?" she screams. "You are older and bigger than she is. You ought to know better. Now, young man, you go right up to your room and get into bed. Debbie, you come with me. You can play with the top in the kitchen while I get dinner."

Thus does the world acquire its dangerous rebels! How could this boy trust his mother or learn to love his sister? Such indignities are never forgotten in a lifetime. How could he be free to learn how to tend to his own business or to cooperate with others when he was dominated by any such forces of jealousy and competition? How could we be surprised to find him a miniature thug at seven who said to his parents, "I hate you" or "I hate Debbie and would like to bash her brains in"?

In cases like this, we are reminded that:

. . . jealousy is cruel as the grave. Its flashes are flashes of fire, a most vehement flame. (Song of Solomon 8:6, R.S.V.)

It is not difficult to see how circumstances and parental misguidance or oversight can combine to foster jealous rivalry. An excess of jealousy always makes a person feel hopeless and leads him, as it did Jimmy, to make an advance toward the rear. Jealous competition never spurs an individual to make his best efforts. It is always a cheat and a fraud because it diverts the mind from the problems to be solved and fastens it on the competitor.

It is a sad fact that most of the jealous competition that exists in families is stirred up because of parents' sincere wish to avoid jealous competition between children. Some of the worst problems in sibling rivalry we have seen have been in families where the parents were determined that their children would love one another—that they would be unselfish and help each other throughout life. Parents, in their anxiety to accomplish this, often defeat their own purposes, and their efforts, in this respect, frequently and unwittingly work in reverse against their own aims.

Parents should maintain their rights as free individuals and should establish that the peace and quiet of their home may not be disturbed by bickering, tattling, quarreling, and jealous complaints, one against another. If children are held *equally* guilty and understand their parents will not support one against another or show any favoritism, they learn to live together on a more tolerant basis. We have developed this theme in greater length in our book *Parents on the Run.**

* *Parents on the Run* (New York: Grosset and Dunlap, 1967).

## 7

## *EVERY CHILD COULD BE A GENIUS*

In our long experience we have found no problem that parents have talked about more consistently than rivalry among their children. They did not, of course, start talking about this in the beginning, but it kept coming up in their conversation. Their descriptions of family life forced us to the conclusion that rivalry is never wholly absent in any family. It stands to reason that rivalry will exist to a certain degree in any family where children have to share the limited facilities of modern life under one roof. Each child, of course, would like to be the only one. Parents should anticipate that any child will play the game of winner-take-all if he can get away with it.

We are convinced that what counts most in this matter is how adults, who live under the same roof with children, handle the problem. With proper parental guidance we have found that children can grow side by side and each find his own potential development. If parents make the mistake of ignoring the early signs of jealous rivalry or of interfering unjustly in favor of one, as Jimmy's mother did, their children can become so entangled in competition as to be emotionally crippled all the rest of their lives unless some intensive re-education halts the crippling.

Children in a family are like seed scattered in a garden. Different varieties of plants grow at different rates of speed. Those that develop the fastest may cast shade on other plants near them. Those in the shade either grow twisted or die in their effort to reach the light above. The fast-growing plants have roots that sap the nourishment and moisture from the soil so that the slower-growing plant is starved for nourishment from below as well as light from above. Every gardener knows that he must see that no plant crowds the others. He must see that each has its own proper place in relation to the others if he wants a maximum yield from his planting. The same is true of members of a family. Each must be free of competition that prevents him from finding his own best development.

Every living thing must struggle for its own survival. It is not selfish to look after oneself. It is the basis of social living. No one should be a burden on another. Our difficulties in life don't stem from the fact that each person seeks his own way of life, property, and fulfillment. Such difficulties arise only when one person insists on taking what belongs rightly to another. It is the problem of mine and thine. The development of children in a family depends on the success of parents in handling this problem of mine and thine. In other words, it all depends on whether the family dissolves into unbridled jealous competition or whether each member learns to mind his own affairs and to do his own job.

Many have thought the endless fighting among children in

the family is a normal factor of family life. They regard the almost constant bickering, tattling, and mutual interference as a part of nature's plan. They are distressed, of course, when the older child clouts the little one on the head, and they thank heaven if Junior isn't done in by the blow. It does not occur to them that this is unnecessary most of the time if the family is properly handled. Some parents encourage children to tattle on each other as a way of knowing what is going on whenever their backs are turned. Or they permit teasing and unpleasant nicknames around the house, believing that it is all in the spirit of good, clean fun. The fact is that such families are hotbeds of jealous competition in which mutual destruction goes on all the while. There are so few families where mutual respect is practiced habitually that we have a distorted view of what is normal.

The objective of family life should be to set up conditions such as a gardener does, so that each individual shapes up into the kind of person his inner nature intended him to be. Each of us brings into this world a gift of nature that's unique, or different from that given to any other, just as each leaf on a tree is different from all others. Goethe, the famous German philosopher, once said, "Every child under six is a genius."

If we watch young children who have not been distracted by the influence of those about them, we see clearly the working of this inner genius. Each seems to seek the kind of "food" that will nourish his inner growth. These trends toward individual development appear at a very early age in such children. But children who have been misled into jealous watchfulness of those around them show mostly signs of heightened irritability and contentiousness. Their inner life is not awakened but instead is pushed aside in favor of fighting the continuous battles they've learned to wage with those nearest them.

Many parents begin almost at the birth of a child to distract him. They seem unable to content themselves with the normal response an infant gives naturally and automatically. Instead, they selfishly seek to stimulate him beyond his needs. How many have you seen leaning over a crib, making goo-goo sounds at a tiny baby. Why can't adults allow a baby the privilege of contacting them when he wishes to—at his own right time and according to his own needs? Isn't it much more important that a baby not lose contact with his inner self and not become alienated from that source of power which lies within him? How unfortunate it is when a child, by the age of one, already shows signs of being a tyrant. How frightening it is to see him so soon aware of his power over the adults in his environment. Then it is he begins to compete for their attention, usually when they have other things they must do. Can we wonder that such a child grows to be demanding and unreasonable?

An adult-centered child can keep any number of adults in a room occupied with him and still be very unhappy in the whole process even though he may succeed in being the center of everyone's attention. We had occasion recently to see a child who had *not* been so distracted. It was such an unusual experience we kept looking for the catch in it! This only shows how seldom one sees a wholly unspoiled infant. He and his parents were strangers to us at the time a friend brought them to visit. There were eight adults in the same room with him for two hours. He was given some toys and fell to work on them. Although in completely strange surroundings, he kept busy and absorbed. Not once did he stop his play or pay attention to what the rest of us were doing. Eventually he got tired and crawled up in his mother's lap to sleep.

This one-year-old boy's physical coordination would have

done credit to a child of three. It was remarkable to watch the imagination he showed in his play. His genius had not been tampered with and he minded his own business completely. He was as yet uncontaminated by an urge to compete against any of the eight people in the room—not even his parents, who sat relaxed and happy the whole while. That was, perhaps, the secret of his success. His parents obviously adored him, but they made no move or gesture to inflict themselves on him. Nor did they try to distract the flow of conversation to focus anyone's attention on their son. He truly seemed as mature as anyone in the room. This is the sensible way animals bring up their babies, and we could learn much from their training methods.

Family life is a delightful experience in those cases where parents and children know how to mind their own affairs. Each member of the family becomes an individual in his own right and develops his own different flavor. Each pursues his own interests without the others making slurs in his direction. They do not imitate each other, nor does one pretend that his own interests and tastes are the only right and good ones. A mild good humor lubricates their contacts with each other. Each one is allowed to have his own little crazy streaks if he so chooses. The others even have a certain pride in seeing that he or any other member of the family is a different kind of person. No one feels that he was sent by God on high to teach the others taste and manners or to make the laws binding the group.

We have had the pleasure of knowing some families of this kind. In one such family of four children, the twelve-year-old boy decided he didn't want to have his hair cut. This happened back in the forties when a boy could still be recognized at a distance by short hair. At that time, no boy could be found wearing long hair. No one in the family knew why

Jonathan didn't want his hair cut, nor did he volunteer to tell any of them. Although his mother was distressed to be sure, she said nothing. After all, it was his hair, not hers. It grew longer and longer. Eventually Jonathan looked like Daniel Boone. No one had the slightest idea when or if he would change his mind and have his hair cut. All the other family members waited with a kind of awe to see if anything would arise which would tempt him. Then came an invitation from a girl to come to her birthday party. She was a pretty little thing. The family waited still without comment.

The day before the party Jonathan approached his mother for money to get his hair cut just as if it had been the most routine thing in his life until now. To this day no one knows why he let his hair grow so long. As a family they did not pry into each other's private motives about such things. As individuals they respected the right to privacy and the right to live unmolested.

The four children in this family are all grown now. Each one has landed solidly on his own feet in a remarkable manner. Each is quite different from the other three. Not one of them has got snarled up in the kind of side show that would waste their lives—as so often happens. The so-called "temptations" did not seem to interest them or beckon them away from the main path of accomplishment. Each became a contributor in his chosen field. They live today, as they grew up, without pushing or pulling, and with no outward or obvious signs of jealous competition.

This type of family life is all too rare. Once a child has the habit of minding the business of the other fellow, it is not easy for him to unlearn it. We, of course, would not presume to catalogue all the "right" things that should be done in a family any more than we would attempt to list all the "wrong" things a family might do. But we have discovered that there is a simple principle that seems to work success-fully. That principle applies to anyone of any age. It is: "Mind your own business and make it unprofitable for those around you if they fail to mind their own business." We have found that when parents operate on this principle there is a climate in the home that encourages self-development and discour-ages any tendency toward meddling in the affairs of others.

It is not the moment-to-moment events in a family that make the over-all effect. It is the over-all atmosphere that determines largely what will happen from moment to mo-ment. The degree of jealous competition seems to be the factor that makes the difference. As long as it is kept low, children feel at home with themselves and others.

# 8

# A "CLOSE" FAMILY

The tendency to rivalry is a part of the survival urge itself. The extent and direction of its development is largely due to the way children are managed in a family, as we have seen. We have found some of the most unbridled jealous competition and crippling in families that consider themselves "close."

In such families no one minds his own business. This is apparent in the conversation of the members of the family. They seldom have anything else to talk about except what this or that member of the family thinks, says, or does. The tragedy is that they believe they are devoted to each other. They announce this in lofty tones as if to say that anyone not born into this family is somehow of a lesser order of being. They really believe they are held together by a deep love for each other. And they are just as certain that they want only the best of good fortune for each other.

When they mention their family they mean the whole clan of blood relations both dead and alive! In the living members one finds no traces of independence. Any who have developed self-determination got out long ago to follow their own destiny. And when any have had such effrontery the other members of the family drop the pretense of loving interest and begin back-biting and gossiping about them. Thus do they give themselves away, because this makes it obvious that the factor that has kept them so tightly knit is not love at all. It is fear that one of them will get ahead of the others too far—socially, financially, or otherwise!

There are many curious things about such families or clans tied in blood relationships. When a member marries, the wife or husband from another family is not regarded as belonging to the clan. He or she remains an outsider. And woe be to the one who does not fall in line with all the rites and observances of the clan. His good behavior will be taken for granted. Any bad behavior will not be forgotten or forgiven. The wife of a clan member is expected to accept all his relatives uncritically and entertain them as she would her most cherished friends. But she is in for a hard time if she invites members of her own family to dine or visit.

There are, of course, degrees and varieties of such close, ever-loving families. Some are not as restrictive of human development as others. But we have found that they form a general pattern of behavior. It is good to know what we may expect of them. The pattern of jealous competition is such that we may expect to find that almost all the members in this type of family will be in rivalry with all the other blood relations. One finds them arguing and bickering about nonessentials—choosing sides and making a federal case out of trivial matters. Thus they tend to set up deadlocks so that no one can get ahead for long. It seems to be a matter of prestige to disagree with each other about anything or everything. Each gives his "good" reasons for what he says or does. And these are always high-minded and noble since each feels he is always on the side of the angels in his view of things. But "good" reasons are never "real" reasons. The real reason in such behavior could only be the will to disagree or jealous competition. This is obvious since each member refuses to play second fiddle. None will give up his bickering long enough to move forward in his own development.

The desire for personal recognition—or to be considered infallible—makes it impossible for one to give up in favor of another. Since their forces become equal and opposite, we find only endless recrimination and mutual blame or fault-finding in such groups. The arguments, as they foment, cannot be resolved by bringing up the facts or by being logical. No one allows himself to be convinced because he dares not yield a point to the one with whom he argues. His prestige, he feels, is on the chopping block!

Families of this type do not follow the laws nature intended. We were never born to stick together on the basis of mutual, infantile competition and watchfulness. Nature intended each to go his own way as soon as he reached physical maturity—for every living thing to struggle for personal fulfillment just as the animals do. The films of animals in their *natural* state, made by such people as Walt Disney or Milo Perkins of the Chicago Zoo, teach us a lot about such matters. They reveal the way animals modify their competitive behavior in different situations. They show that animals do not indulge in blind interpersonal competition even though they are not supposed to be able to think things out.

The birds, for instance, have what is called "pecking rights." When a flock of birds finds scattered food, they settle on the ground with a certain amount of space around each one. The distance is about the length of the extended neck. The food in that area immediately surrounding each one belongs to him. If his neighbor gets greedy and tries to peck outside his space he gets pecked on the head for his ill manners!

In the jungle there is an accepted order of protocol for a banquet after a lioness has made her kill. She steps aside until the male has eaten his fill before she begins to eat. When she has had all she wants, she allows the babies to have their dinner. When they have finished, the jackals move in on the carcass to eat. And what is left on the bones remains for the vultures that have been circling about awaiting their turn.

The behavior of African animals during a serious drought is probably the most amazing thing of all. The small water holes dry up and all the animals are obliged to congregate around a few larger holes where water is still available. At such times varieties of known "natural enemies" are to be found drinking almost side by side. Since they show no jealous competition at these times, it would appear that they have a live-and-let-live arrangement about such matters. Even the carnivores do not prey on other animals' need of water for survival. They do not kill until they have moved back into the surrounding country.

These brief observations show that the behavior among animals differs from the sometimes unbridled interpersonal competitive behavior among human beings. Men have been known to corner the market on wheat or some other basic commodity that is needed and keep it from those who cannot afford to buy it. And the kind of mass murder committed by Hitler would be unknown in the animal world. Animals do not seem to employ trickery or deceit to destroy each other in the way humans do.

At this point we are reminded of the Biblical story of Esau and Jacob. They were the twin sons of Isaac and Rebekah.

The first to be born was called Esau; he had hair all over his body. Then his brother was born, and they called him Jacob. Isaac was sixty years old when Rebekah bore these twins. And it is written:

When the boys grew up, Esau was a skilful hunter, a man of the field, while Jacob was a quiet man, dwelling in tents. Isaac loved Esau, because he ate of his game; but Rebekah loved Jacob. (Genesis 25: 27, 28, R.S.V.)

Esau was to get his father's inheritance. He was entitled to the birthright because he was the elder. And when Isaac became blind and was about to die, he planned to bestow the right of succession on Esau before it was too late. He asked Esau to kill an animal and make a stew. Isaac promised, after he had eaten it, to grant his blessing on Esau. Rebekah overheard Isaac make this promise. She wanted her favored son, Jacob, to get his father's inheritance. So when Esau went hunting she confided what she had heard to Jacob and plotted with him as to how they could outwit the old blind Isaac.

Esau had hairy hands whereas Jacob's were smooth. So the mother sent Jacob out to kill a lamb and put the skin on the back of his hands. Then she cooked the lamb and made a stew of it. Jacob presented it to his father before Esau returned with the venison. When Isaac heard Jacob's voice, he suspected a plot and asked, as the mother had known he would, to feel the back of his hands. Feeling the hair, Isaac was convinced and gave Jacob his blessing in the belief that he was giving it to his favorite son. He said, "The voice is Jacob's voice, but the hands are the hands of Esau." This saying remains as the symbol of trickery and deceit even today. In this respect man is the only animal that lays traps for his brother man. This is a kind of cannibalism and competitiveness unknown among other animals.

# 9

## COMPETITION VERSUS COOPERATION

There are many who argue, "Where would we be if it weren't for competition?" And they point to Darwin's theory of evolution in the belief that nature uses competition to further survival of the species. It is true that one of the laws of nature is *self*-survival and that animals have fought each other for food or sex if the supply was limited. There is no doubt that as a result certain organisms did die out and others took their place in the world. This is what Darwin referred to as the "survival of the fittest." That is true; the fittest did survive. Those creatures that could remain *productive* and *adaptable* to the *problems* they had to face managed to survive. They met the demands by growing and developing according to the needs of the situation, but not by fighting against other species in a kind of jealous contest as some people believe.

The fittest for survival of any species is the one that can

59

keep on the job and meet the needs of the situation. It is destructive nonsense to believe that jealous interpersonal competition promotes survival. Survival and growth, in our case, depend on the exchange of goods for goods. All life and nature itself must maintain a profitable balance of forces. As humans we survive only if we remain productive. The patriarchs who wrote the Bible recognized this, for in the Old ·Testament it is written that God gave Adam and Eve the command to be fruitful.

Man has yet to make up his mind whether he does or doesn't approve of competition. From one side of his mouth he praises it and urges it on the young. Then, out of the other corner, he condemns it roundly and scolds the young for competing. In one breath he insists that competition is the life of trade; in the next he petitions the legislature to set up tariffs in order to restrict or completely eliminate competition. Or companies form giant mergers to stop all competition down the line. One moment we say winning is all that counts. The next moment we are demanding cooperation and teamwork from people we urged to win at any price. The quandary at the heart of things is: do we or don't we want it? Is it or isn't it good for us?

Though we may speak of friendly competition, it exists only at the language level. At the behavior level, no such thing exists. Competition is always hostile; its goal is power to rule and dominate—to win. The object of competition is to eliminate and destroy our opposition so all the profit is ours. With this in mind, let's visualize what would happen if we could always fix the game in sports. If only one team wins all the games, who would want to bother to watch the sport? Besides, what point would there be in the opposition continuing to play the game? We can see it stops being a game if jealous competition reaches the point at which winning all the games becomes the one and only important issue.

The only enjoyment of so-called competitive sports is when the various players are artist-players. It is a joy and an inspiration to see what can be done by a human being in that instance. It opens our eyes to ways for our own improvement. Artist-players work together as a *team*. Their object is more like the efforts of a fine ballet company. Each wants to discover the beauty that is possible when he does his own job to its ultimate perfection. The work of each contributes to the whole effort. Together they produce the maximum effectiveness with the greatest efficiency. But what happens if there's a solo player on the team? The solo player is moved by his jealousy to prevent anyone from scoring—even the members of his own team.

We once watched a game with a whole field full of solo players. This occurred in an institution maintained for juvenile delinquents.

There was no recreation program for the boys in this institution. They didn't fly kites, play ball, or do anything else together. The staff insisted that it was useless to try to get the boys to play ball or anything as a group. We refused to believe this story until we saw for ourselves what happened in such a situation. For our benefit the staff took the boys out on the field and threw them a mask, gloves, balls, and bats. There was a mad scramble among the boys to grab anything they could lay hands on. Those who managed to get hold of anything dashed wildly in all directions with the others chasing them to get their loot away from them. Not one of them would listen to the voices of the staff members who were trying to give them instructions. Every single child on that field was lost in jealous competition with every other child. It was not possible to organize any kind of give-and-take relationship with them. These children, young as they were, had already failed in life. They couldn't even play together.

It reminded us of Lewis Carroll's description of the Queen's croquet game in *Alice in Wonderland:* "Alice soon come to the conclusion that it was a very difficult game. The players all played at once, without waiting for turns. . . . 'I don't think they play at all fairly,' Alice began, in a rather complaining tone, 'and they all quarrel so dreadfully one can't hear oneself speak—and they don't seem to have any rules in particular; at least, if there are, nobody attends to them. . . .'"

Cooperative effort may be of two varieties. The most frequent is the type that exists between the butcher, the baker, and the candlestick maker. Each of them performs his own function to the best of his ability. Their hours of operation are not the same and their skills are different. They may or may not feel personally friendly to each other. But each is responsible for the excellence of his own product and fulfills himself in its production. He is a cooperator because he makes a necessary contribution to the whole.

Another form of cooperation is that associated in our minds with the Volga boatmen who had to pull on their oars in precise unison with their fellow oarsmen to propel the boat forward. Today this type of cooperative effort survives chiefly among the members of college crews whose rhythmic synchronization is beautiful to see.

Neither of these types of cooperation demands that the participants be friendly with the others on a personal basis. All that is necessary is that each does his own job at the right time.

Most people mistake conformity for cooperation. We must not expect everyone to march to the same drumbeat. Conformity is mutual enslavement. It is the destruction of cooperation. Conformity prevents individual contribution and self-realization.

Doing things together may or may not be cooperation, nor is helping others necessarily cooperation. The baker must set his dough and bake his bread at night to be ready to supply his customers in the morning, whereas the candlestick maker may work at any hour as long as he has his product available on demand. If the butcher and candlestick maker insisted on helping the baker, the whole scheme of things would be upset and the bread would probably be inferior as a result.

Each cooperator must be free to satisfy his own needs first. He will not be able to accomplish his function if he is hobbled by the need to please others first. We please others best when we have done our own job to the fullest of our capacity. We serve ourselves and them least when we merely "go along" on any other basis.

Much unhappiness arises among people when they have a mistaken concept of cooperation. They may be tempted or persuaded to "go along" on ventures and fail to maintain their own initiative. In that case they would be failing to fulfill their own function without truly adding anything to the situation. They would have deprived themselves without enriching others. And by "going along" against their inner will and judgment they would feel a basic resentment against the one with whom they cooperated in a mistaken way.

Cooperation is never similar to mutual enslavement. The end result should be individual self-realization.

# 10

# JEALOUS REACTIVITY

Now it is time to discuss a particular type of jealous competition which we've come to call "courtship dancing." It is a prevalent and highly irritating form of noncooperation. The courtship dancer is always trying to throw others off their course and prevent them from going forward on their own initiative. He has lost his own direction in life because of his habit of jealous competition and tries to latch onto those around him as if they should stop work and be his dancing partner. To get the full implication of such useless activity, we must draw a sharp picture of mental health against which to compare the full tragedy of the courtship dancer.

Mental health depends on the ability of an individual to keep his own show on the road, regardless of what other attractions or distractions are being offered in competing side shows next to him. He must maintain his own center of gravity if he is to remain productive and sane. No one of us, of course, manages to hold his equilibrium and judgment all the while. We are all tempted far too often to be influenced by our neighbor more than is good for us. As Emerson wrote in his "Essay on Self-Reliance," "I am ashamed to think how easily we capitulate to badges and names, to large societies and dead institutions. Every decent and well-spoken individual affects and sways me more than is right. I ought to go upright and vital, and speak the rude truth in all ways."

What Emerson is saying is that jealous competition distracts us from our own genius and delivers us like helpless captives to any outside influence that happens to catch our fancy. As a matter of fact, our personal susceptibility to such outside influence is the yardstick by which we are measured by others and may measure ourselves as well.

The habit of getting hopelessly caught up in and reacting to the opinion of the other fellow is what we call courtship dancing. Rightly speaking, courtship dancing is only for the birds. It is a term coined by ornithologists, to describe the mating habits of certain African jungle fowl. They pivot around each other during courtship or dance back and forth across and in front of each other. The male uses this technique to make a good impression on the female. The jealous person does the same to distract those around him.

The type of obstruction that is set up in the courtship dance often reminds us of two people who get caught in a doorway trying to pass each other. Instead of each one passing on his right, they begin jumping sideways until one of them has sense enough to stop it. We can easily recognize the same mutual obstruction in the jealous bickering of children. We know a family in which the two children carried rulers to the table to measure each slice of meat down to the last sixteenth of an inch so they could be sure one didn't get a bigger piece than the other. These children certainly weren't starving for meat. They were engaged in courtship dancing. It was the Cain-and-Abel routine to determine which one was the favored child in the sight of the parents.

The problems of life demand independent activity and judgment for their solution. Without activity, we fail. But courtship dancing isn't activity; it's reactivity, or minding the other fellow's business instead of our own. The person who minds his own business remains active all day long; the competitive type remains reactive all day long. The mature person follows a straight path to his goal. The immature person goes around in circles; he circles the person who is the target of his jealousy at the moment and he can't get along to his own affairs.

There are many who are so accustomed to reactivity that they accept it as normal behavior. Perhaps none of us is free from being reactive about certain things although in most matters we may behave actively and independently. Almost everyone has his jealous moments! But he should learn how to separate the sheep from the goats. If we train ourselves to recognize the difference between activity and reactivity, we can at least watch the wheels as they go round. And it is pretty important that we do when one considers that "though the mills of God grind slowly, yet they grind exceeding small."

It is easy to learn to recognize reactivity. For one thing it smacks of infantilism. Haven't you noticed that a person in a jealous tantrum always looks childish? He acts as if he were a weak child, unable to help himself by any constructive means. He can't see the road ahead because he imagines it is blocked by the person he's jealous of. Then, too, jealous reactivity makes a person very imitative—a "monkey see, monkey do" kind of person. Such a type is often referred to as "keeping up with the Joneses." This makes for a sterile, destructive condition not unlike slavery. It keeps a person minding and interfering with the other fellow's business. While he does that, he is not free to tend to his own affairs or to see the productive thing to do. In our mirror, it reflects itself as "working for others all day long without being on their payroll."

The person who is *not* reactive, on the other hand, can be recognized by his independence. The definition of independence is "freedom from outside government and outside support." This is the same as being self-employed. The active person doesn't turn to anyone to prompt his thinking or dictate his actions. He is neither obedient nor disobedient to those around him. Instead, he evaluates the situation and follows his own best guess as to how to solve the confronting problem, whatever it is. Then he acts. He is free and productive. He keeps his own show on the road.

Let's think of it another way. Let's think of each of us as being similar to a company with a hundred shares of stock. If each owned the whole hundred shares, he would be mighty lucky and all the profit would be his. But in this world of high finance, someone else usually owns a few shares of our stock and they collect their dividends from us according to the amount of our stock they hold. We can remain independent, productive, and in control of our own affairs just as long as we keep at least fifty-one per cent of all the stock. No one can vote us out of control while we hang onto the majority of the stock.

If we have the majority of the stock, we can set the policy and the direction of our activity without being blocked. The control lies "inside us" or we might say that the center of gravity does. That is, we are inwardly directed. The center of gravity would lie "outside us" if we were to sell our shares to those around us and end up having less than fifty per cent of our own stock. We would have to submit to the conditions and influence of those outsiders who held the majority of our stock. This is what happens to the person with the habit of jealous reactivity. He is only a minority stockholder in his own affairs and is constantly voted down by those around him. His courtship dancing is only a futile effort to regain the control he no longer has—and can't regain by any such dancing routine. He would like to liquidate them. No doubt about it—there's no peace for a man in debt to outside creditors.

Let us consider this in the light of marriage or other partnerships. Is it possible to maintain one's center of gravity in such relationships? Can the other partner maintain his simultaneously? The first thing to consider is that no relationship justifies anyone's abdicating his full responsibility in a situation. Nor does anyone have the right to make another person responsible for his welfare. So, in a marriage or other partnership, each should keep fifty-one percent of his own initiative. If one partner makes the mistake of abdicating in favor of the other partner, he does so to escape personal responsibility so that he may blame the other when things go wrong. Partnership does not sanctify the abdication of personal integrity. A relationship that demands subordination of either partner should be dissolved, since it will degenerate into a dominance-submission relationship which can only destroy a chance for a healthy, creative, and productive relationship.

When one gets caught playing the role of subordination in marriage or any other partnership, jealousy sets in, and then nothing turns out right because it puts the subordinate one at cross-purposes to the dominant partner. In such a case, a feeling of isolation and loneliness follows. Resentment leads him to sabotage the other partner. He withholds his best efforts and becomes nonproductive to spite his partner. He also becomes a burden and not a help in his effort not only to spite the partner but to inflate his own ego.

Fortunately, a person can free himself from playing a subordinate role if he faces the situation for what it is and learns to understand what has happened—and gets rid of the demands of his hungry ego for its inflation. He then can let go and walk on. One man we remember was able to save his job by letting go. His name was Arnold.

Arnold worked in a branch of an international bank. His work was excellent, and, as a result, he was picked for special training. If he made good, he was to be assigned eventually to go in an official capacity from bank to bank around the world. He was brought to New York City, as the first step in his training, and was started at the bottom. Estimates arrived on his desk. He had to check the figures and then approve them. After that, they were passed to a man at a desk next to him whose responsibility was to double-check. He was overawed in the beginning by the faster pace of the new office and he was afraid that he might not "gain grace in the sight of his lords." Well, he didn't!

Arnold's mind was occupied with making a good impression instead of checking for mistakes as it should have been. He had almost never made mistakes before. Now he began to make them frequently. The man next to him pounced on each one. He also went out of his way to humiliate this new employee when he passed papers back to him. A jungle dance began. What could you expect?

Our friend, Arnold, determined to check and double-check each thing to make sure nothing was wrong before he passed the papers to his neighbor. But no one succeeds in chasing two rabbits at once without loving one and despising the other. His job demanded accuracy but his hurt feelings demanded that he rescue his tattered ego. He was devoting more and more of his creative energy to the defense of his ego but sacrificing his accuracy, since one can't do both things simultaneously. His main goal was to get his tormentor off his back.

He began to be aware that he would like to murder this dancing partner of his. By this time his superiors were finding fault with him. He had nightmares that he would be sent back to the bush league before he even had a chance to come to bat at all. He was terrified. He felt like an outcast in a field where he had only recently been one of the chosen ones.

He woke up to his situation before it was too late. He was shocked to realize the condition similar to hypnosis that had gradually come over him. He saw how he had slipped into a murderous rage against his brother worker and how he had been destroying himself in the process of hating the other man. He realized that it had all come about when he began making jealous comparisons between himself and those around him so that his mind had wandered off his own business. Now Arnold could see the vicious circle that had closed around him as he got more and more into jungle dancing with his partner. As soon as his eyes opened to his reactive situation, he immediately pulled himself out of the tailspin by stopping his jealous comparisons at once. With his mind now free for his own affairs, the whole difficulty passed without further trouble.

Arnold's case reminds us again of the story of Cain and Abel. When they brought to the Lord their offerings, the Lord had regard for Abel's but not for Cain's. So Cain was very angry and his countenance fell (the look of jealousy).

The Lord said to Cain, "Why are you angry, and why has your countenance fallen? If you do well, will you not be accepted? And if you do not well sin is couching at the door; its desire is for you, but you must master it." (Genesis 4: 6, 7, R.S.V.)

## 11

## *HYPERSENSITIVITY*

Hypersensitivity is another mask for jealous competition. The hypersensitive person is a vain person who constantly makes invidious comparisons as to whether he is more valued or held in greater esteem than others. Since he secretly believes that he and his wishes should be so considered, he weighs and measures the number of compliments that come his way and the real or fancied slights he gets. One might say he acts as if his secret wishes and sensitive feelings should be as laws binding on others. This leads him to be not only a jealous but an irritable person who lives on the defensive, ready to attack any trivial or imagined offenses. Let us consider a few examples of how the hypersensitive person expects everyone to weigh all words on a jeweler's scale.

One young man we know was invited to spend the weekend in the country with his girl friend and her family. He had not known the girl long, but already they were much interested in each other and he looked forward to meeting her parents. For him the weekend turned out to be a pleasant one, and there were no clouds on the horizon as far as he could see. As he was leaving he tried to express his appreciation to his hostess, "I have enjoyed myself so much," he began. Before he could finish, the girl's mother exposed her jealousy and hypersensitivity by interrupting him with, "Well, young man, I do hope you will come back some time when you can enjoy *us!*"

Another example of the same trait is a young lady who was so vain and thin-skinned that she kept losing one job after another until she learned to stop pointing her ears and eyes. No sooner would Sarah get a job than she would imagine someone else wanted it or that her boss was definitely trying to undermine her. She was fired from one job before she had a chance to learn all her new duties. The reason for this was that she started the job with the conviction that her boss did nothing but look at the back of her neck all the time. Her discomfort grew by leaps and bounds. She got so she couldn't think of anything but the hot spot on the back of her neck. She made so many mistakes as a result and such a backlog of work piled up on her desk, she became a serious bottleneck and her boss had to let her go. In this particular instance, Sarah's boss did have a desk behind hers, but he had more important things to do than sit and concentrate on the back of his secretary's neck. He was a kind man and he would have been willing to help this girl learn her new duties and keep her job if she hadn't worked up such a conviction that he was her enemy, and if she hadn't been so unapproachable.

Human association is painfully tense and difficult for hypersensitive people. They seem to allow nothing to go unnoticed or unchallenged. They behave as if they had a real allergy to people. It is not too wide of the mark to refer to them as allergic. Haven't you noticed the physical allergies that frequently flourish and abound in such types? To be sure, not everyone who is sensitive and vain expresses it through physical allergies. On the other hand, the victim of allergies is apt to be hypersensitive!

Ulcers, colitis, asthma, and a whole zoo parade of other such disorders may afflict these types. Their physical symptoms seem to flare up or subside pretty much in direct ratio to the amount of jungle dancing they do. We are reminded at this point of Abel's sudden death in the Garden of Eden. Suppose Cain hadn't lost his temper as he did and these two brothers had gone on living side by side, continuing their hypersensitivity to each other. Would Cain have developed an allergy to the meat and wool Abel produced? And would Abel have developed colitis every time he ate a carrot or some cabbage Cain had grown?

We once worked with a vain young burglar about seventeen years old. Tony hadn't developed a physical allergy but he had a certain emotional symptom that was equally embarrassing to him. His symptom was nonreading. He couldn't read a word. At the time of our involvement in his case, he had been picked up for his second burglary offense and committed to a psychiatric ward for study. Should he be excused a second time? Ought he to be sent to prison for his crime? Or did he need some kind of remedial help so that he could develop into an honest, productive person? These were the questions. In Tony's case, there seemed good reason to follow the latter course. The first time he was picked up the authorities hadn't discovered that he couldn't read. This time they decided to see if he would straighten himself out if they gave him a chance to learn to read.

Solomon once said, "Vanity of vanities, . . . all is vanity." Well, our young burglar, Tony, was the vainest of people. Every hair on his head was in place. In a mod kind of way, he looked like a fashion advertisement. At least, everyone else looked shabby by comparison. He was shy beyond belief, and one could only wonder how he ever got up courage enough to burglarize a store in the first place. He was so much more like a mouse than a lion. It was difficult to get him into any conversation about anything at the beginning. Whenever his inability to read was mentioned he turned pale and cringed as if he'd been hit. One got the impression he'd almost rather hang than let any of his pals or anyone else, for that matter, know he couldn't read. This was his guilty secret and he imagined, in his vanity, that it was his undoing.

All through school Tony had been ashamed. Efforts to teach him had ended in dismal failure. He used to pray to the Holy Virgin that he would wake up the next morning able to read a book—that a miracle might happen in answer to his prayer. The next morning he would eagerly pick up a book only to decipher nothing in its pages. Then he would become bitter against the Virgin for withholding the answer to his prayer. He was pushed from class to class as he grew older, even though he couldn't do any academic work.

More and more his main concern was to hide this gruesome deficiency. He pretended to those who did not know him that all was well with him. When Tony was finally old enough to leave school and get a job, the real trouble broke out. When he applied somewhere for a job and was given an application to fill out, he would pretend he didn't want the job after all and walk out. It is not surprising, is it, that finally there wasn't much left to do but for him to begin to steal? After all, he had his fine appearance to keep up, and that cost money. And he had to be able to hold up his head with his gang and prove to them that he was a big shot. Burglary provided a way for him to keep up in the competition. There was nothing left to do, he thought.

When Tony was picked up this second time he had to make a choice: either learn to read or go to jail. He feared both, but learning to read seemed less threatening than a jail sentence, so he agreed to try. Right there we ran into a block. He would not carry a book with him anywhere lest some member of his gang see it and guess his guilty secret. Books for beginners in reading are not the kind that a vainglorious big shot carries on his person!

Then we had an inspiration and decided to type a few limericks on scrap paper for each lesson. He could memorize these and afterward study the face of each word in privacy at his leisure. This he agreed would be safe enough to do. If his gang found them on him, he realized that he could pretend to read what he had only memorized.

It was only a matter of a few months with other such simple reading matter before Tony had picked up enough words to follow and understand a story in a baseball magazine. He was elated. Soon he was confident enough to try other reading material. There was no need to worry any more. The Virgin had answered his prayer at last—but not until after Tony had given up enough of his sensitivity to face his problem and do something constructive about it to help himself.

As we have so often experienced, seven wild horses can't hold a person back once he has experienced success in an area where he had previously tasted only bitter defeat. And, as far as we know, Tony is working now and getting paid for it.

In summary, we have tried to show that the hypersensitive person not only engages in jealous comparison but that hypersensitivity is a thin skin that barely covers a hostile demand for special favors and attention from others. Others are expected to abide by the wishes of a hypersensitive person or suffer his displeasure—even his tyranny.

## 12

## POSSESSIVENESS

Poor Jane! She worked for everyone without being on their payroll. She was twenty-eight and still single. The problems of love and marriage gnawed at her. The males suitable as a husband for her were thinning out under the onslaught of more successful maidens. In a few more years she would have only the culls from which to choose. Like so many girls in a comparable situation, Jane woke up in cold sweats at night worrying about her future. She was desperate to find somebody to marry but she couldn't seem to stumble onto the right guy. She had no awareness as to what was really wrong.

A successful marriage demands a "give" as well as a "take." As Shakespeare said, "There's beggary in the love that can be reckon'd." As far as Jane was concerned, she was a miser when it came to giving anything of herself to anyone, as are all jealously watchful and competitive people. They block themselves even in the approach to finding a partner. They are not only emotionally penurious but behave toward others with a more or less hidden, fighting attitude. Certainly, a courtship puts a great strain on them. They are given to spoiling their contacts before they have time to ripen into anything.

Jane had several brothers against whom she had competed all of her life. Her brothers all married and left her to live alone with her mother. There was a miserable relationship between them. They constantly interfered in each other's business. But let Jane tell us her own story. We shall see how she competes against all those around her.

I am often depressed for days. I'm always nervous and can't sleep well. Since I was a child I've not really enjoyed going out with others. I get angry at small things although big things don't bother me as much. Sometimes I get hysterical and take it out on my mother. When it's all over, I can't remember what it was all about. She is a very bossy woman. I give in too much to her. Everyone treats me just as if I were a child.

The cat is out of the bag already. Jane wants the privileges of a child but she fights back if any responsibility is expected of her. There is evidence in her hysteria that she carries on a jungle dance with her mother. They compete with each other, each struggling to be the boss and to dominate the other. They have become allergic to each other. Well, what could one expect if a young girl sits home with her mother while she envies all the young lovers in her crowd who are out together? This in itself is a temptation to start some thing to pass time away and ease the pain of jealousy and self-pity.

Whenever I'm in new situations, I freeze in front of strangers and get tongue-tied.

The very root of stage fright is jealous competition. She wants to dominate, we can be sure, and make a good impression in all situations. This is too much for anyone to ask. She fears risking exposure, as there is no guarantee that she'll be treated as a special person. People generally are not inclined to grant us such a wish. So she remains at home.

Everyone urges me to get married but I am afraid. I want to travel. If I try to make friends, I go overboard and get kicked for my efforts. I get jealous easily. As a matter of fact, I got jealous when my brother was born.

Jane "multiplieth words without knowledge." She doesn't know how much she is revealing. Of course she doesn't have any friends because she competes against everyone. Jealous people can easily get hurt feelings and turn any social gathering into a tense situation. They hope they will find an answer in travel—that strangers will be kinder than those at home.

At the present time, I hate all men. I want to be something important—like an actress.

We could have guessed this would be her ambition. To be the center of attention is always the goal of rivalry. As an important actress she feels she would be noticed everywhere she went.

It has taken me a whole year to get over a love affair. I met a clean-cut man, but he was not interested in girls. I couldn't twist him around my little finger—like I have most fellows. He said he loved me but he gave all his money to his mother. I didn't like her. So, finally, I broke off with him.

Well, the best way to avoid marriage is for a girl to pick a mother-bound man. Then she can jungle dance both with him and his mother. She can try jealously to come between them and have scenes with him about the "other woman."

Such men usually stick with their mothers, as might be expected. Since a jealous girl can make life difficult, they prefer to cling to a mother who has pampered them. So, faced with a stalemate, Jane broke off and sulked for a year in jealous rage.

My parents always fought. I would take my mother's side and then my father would fight with me. He ran around with other women. Our whole family fought each other all the time. I often wished I had a gun.

Nothing is so contagious in a family as jealous competition. It comes as no surprise that they all fought each other. Nor is it surprising that Jane feared domination by men. Her father and her brothers gave her plenty of competition in the struggle for first place. In this home, there was no picture of cooperation in marriage or in social life within the family.

I had a girl friend for a while, but we were at each other all the while. I avoid such friendships now and going out much because all people do is mind each other's business.

People who are caught in a jealousy trap always accuse others of not being able to mind their own business. How could they know so much about what other people are doing unless they were always watching other people's business themselves? In this respect, they are oblivious of the obvious.

Another reason I avoid parties is because I push myself to be the life of the party. I do things so I'll be considered very entertaining. It is exhausting for me when I do that. It is such hard work. I can't even relax at a dance where there are all good dancers.

Unless she dominates in all respects, any event is ruined. So, we can see how she can spoil an evening for herself simply because "they are all good dancers."

My main fear is that I will marry a man who will mistreat me. It makes me ill when I think of it.

Well, now, isn't this a wonderful image to have in your mind when you go to a party or a dance, especially if you want to find a man to marry!

I feel miserable today. I got an invitation for a dance at the Astoria but I won't go. All my friends and everyone else will be better dressed than I. I can't afford an expensive dress and I refuse to go if I can't be equal to others.

Is she so all-wise she can know that everyone at the dance will be dressed better than she? Of course not. But jealous competition obliges her to imagine that all others will be preferred to her. Feeling unsure of dominating the whole scene, she prefers to stay home and feel sorry for herself.

A man recently got interested in me but he is more intellectual than I am. That's why he doesn't introduce me to his friends. Everyone loves him. He likes my mother and they visit together. All he wants of me is to go to bed. I think he is jealous of me. He says I don't trust him.

She can't stand the fact that other people like this man. It bothers her to think he is more intellectual than she is. She wonders, no doubt, how he can enjoy talking to her mother. The very things that make this man attractive to her or to others seem to be a source of pain to her. She puts him in the position of being "damned if he does and damned if he doesn't." We can imagine that this relationship will go no better than all the others Jane has had. If he asks her to marry him, it will be worse. The competition and jealousy will only sharpen. For she is the kind of girl that Dr. Adler, our teacher, once discussed. When someone told him that a girl like Jane had married, his reply was, "Against whom?" And this man of Jane's—should he marry her—might have occasion to agree with Oscar Wilde, who said, "In this world there are only two tragedies. One is not getting what one wants, and the other is getting it."

Jane's story helps us to see how the hot breath of jealous competition sets up a climate that withers whatever grows in it. For her and others like her, there is little hope unless they come to understand the mistakes they make and retrain themselves to mind their own affairs rather than habitually struggling and comparing themselves with everyone around them. When they fail to do this, they create the hell in which they live.

## 13

## MARRIAGE IS NOT A LICENSE
## TO EXPLOIT

Martha was a fine-looking woman past middle age, well dressed and cultured. Her husband had died and her children had grown up and gone out into the world. She had an independent income, but her life seemed empty and she was lonely. Then she met a presentable professional man, and after a relatively short courtship they were married. That was when the trouble began.

During the courtship, this man had plied Martha with flowers, candy, books, and endless telephone calls as well as every other attention. This had pleased her, and she did not have any realization that it might be a sign of a highly possessive, controlling personality in the man. Such suitors usually collect their fee by expecting that you deny them nothing. It wasn't long after marriage before she discovered that her new husband was very stingy with his money and felt she ought to pay all her own expenses. The kind of attentions he had given her were withdrawn, but he wanted her attention all the time.

After many tense arguments, they found an uneasy truce regarding financial matters whereby she got a minimum sum from him for household expenses. That was bad enough, but, in the meantime, a more disturbing factor had arisen. He became obsessed with the idea that Martha was trying to attract the attention of other men. She dared not look to the right or left if they went out to dinner or driving together because he would make violent accusations and scenes.

For a while, Martha tried to reason with him to prove to him that she had interest in no one but him. He would calm down and "forgive" her, as if she had somehow damaged or betrayed him. But the scenes became more frequent rather than less. She began to lose all her spontaneity and happiness in life. If she went visiting without him, he managed to phone to check whether she was there or not. She felt like a prisoner who was condemned and denied any way of proving her innocence of crime. She tried desperately to find a way to handle the situation so that he would not get jealous. But the more she tried, the worse it got for her. In short, she did not realize that any effort to justify oneself to another person only serves to give that person more power to dominate and enslave. There is no such thing as a little jealousy; it is an all-out effort to destroy the object of its envy. Like the Trojan horse, it attacks the part as an excuse to destroy the whole.

Numberless marriage partners are afflicted in this way. They usually make the mistake of believing that this is sexual interest or sexual jealousy. They almost never see the coherence of the total behavior of their mate. The person given to the habit of jealous competition expresses it in countless areas, if not in all areas of his life. This habit respects few, if any, limits. The person who is bitten by it approaches every situation as if he were in great danger of being put back, overlooked, or defrauded. Such persons act as if they had been born impoverished, had lived poor, and were fearful of dying poor unless they fought for every little advantage. All others appear in their eyes as competitors who will get the better of the deal. They must be watchful at all times and trust no one. Their jealous disposition spoils every relationship, including their sexual life.

But what if his wife *is* interested in looking around at other men? Or worse still, perhaps she is actively thinking of making conquests on the side? Or what if she is even planning to leave him the first chance she gets? The answer is substantially the same. He still has no right to oppress her by his jealousy. No one can hold another person against his will. If he honestly believes that she is unworthy or unfair in the relationship, then it is up to him to do something *constructive* about *his own situation* and not depend on her. He has no right to be destructive of her as he has chosen to be in this case. If he is convinced she endangers his welfare or his integrity, then he should not live with her. There is no excuse for anyone living with another if he thinks that person is dishonest and intends to habitually degrade him. That would not be good for society nor for those living together in this manner. It would point to a defect in his own character if he were a party to such an arrangement and would not be a fault of hers alone. The responsibility for the matter would rest with him. No one should regard another person as the "cause" of his behavior. Only a habit of jealous dependence could lead a person to use another's actions as a justification for his own behavior.

The habit of jealous dependence goes all the way back to the childhood of Tom. It did not begin when he got married.

And, for this reason, it couldn't be handled simply as a marriage problem. His wife had begun to suspect this fact. From relatives of his she found out, after she had married him, that his first wife had been constantly oppressed in the very same way. Her response had been to live a mouselike existence with no outside expression of her own other than bringing up their children. She had had a miserable life as a result.

The second wife, however, had no intention of giving up her integrity in such a manner or of living perpetually under a cloud of jealous doubt as if she were a criminal. As the pattern of Tom's behavior became clearer, she made up her mind not to live as a "second-class citizen" the way his first wife had. She decided that she would no longer make any effort to justify herself in his eyes even if it ended their relationship. In other words, she was willing to live honestly with him in full equality but not as an inferior who had to be constantly watched and checked. As long as he behaved as a friend rather than a jailor or a judge, she determined to stay with him.

There is seldom much else that can be done except to maintain full independence in the face of any such jealous habit of mind that has been so long ingrained. In such situations, we have to learn to plow a straight furrow and to know what we intend to do on each occasion that arises. Otherwise, we are led into defensive reactive behavior without end. We are trapped in a courtship dance, occupied and enslaved.

What can be expected from this second wife's decision? It all depends on whether she does maintain her independence. If her husband realizes that she will not live with him in the face of any further jealous scenes, he will be obliged to "fish or cut bait" about his own situation. When he finds he can no longer tyrannize, it might lead him to seek counsel as to how to overcome the problem of his jealousy. That could be the beginning of a new life for Tom. He might become emotionally mature rather than remain an immature, demanding individual who wants always to be given special privileges and assurances in life.

If, on the other hand, he cannot face his own problem of jealousy, then he must live alone in his own misery as best he can. At least his wife will not be destroyed or undermined in her morale on this basis. Marriage is not a license for either partner systematically to exploit or oppress the other partner. It is intended as a union of two equal, independent, mature, constructive individuals who are both willing to pull their own weight in the contract. When there is jealousy in the relationship, it demands more than its share of rights and eventually destroys the relationship.

It is not often that we find such a self-reliant person as this second wife trapped into marriage with such a jealous partner. More often it is a case of both partners being leaning, dependent types, each expecting the other one to carry him piggyback in some important detail of life. This sort of arrangement amounts to mutual exploitation. It is as if one said, "I will pay your bills and maintain you only if you will surrender any will of your own." And the other says, "I dare not stand on my own feet and will sell my identity to you for your mess of pottage!" In such arrangements, however, it unfortunately happens that each complains bitterly about the other, that the price they pay is too high.

The only defense possible for us against attacks made by the jealously competitive is to stand alone and not be tempted into efforts at self-justification. We should not allow ourselves to be drawn into the jungle dance they wish to start with us. We can't prevent the jealous person from seeing the world through his bent and twisted spectacles, if he insists on having such a vision. That is his misfortune, and our efforts to placate him will only feed his desire for further assurances on our part. That isn't the way to help him—or ourselves. If our vision is straight, let that be enough for us. We must remember that he doesn't want us to prove our innocence but rather wants our submission to him. To grant that would mean a part of us must die. And that would not be right for us, for him, or for the world around us. If we made that mistake, everyone would be the loser.

## 14

## BOASTFUL ALCOHOLICS

"Alcohol is my problem." That's what every alcoholic says. And he believes that is the problem he has to lick. Most other people share this belief—that the demon rum has to be routed if the heavy drinker is to be helped. We might believe it ourselves had it not been for two years' experience in an alcoholic clinic, where we learned to know the alcoholic temperament. We found the main problem of every alcoholic to be jealous competition—the central core of his whole difficulty. The only time treatment is effective, in our estimation, is when the alcoholic becomes less hypersensitive and competitive. This strong affinity between liquor and jealous competition needs to be understood by both the alcoholic and those who deal with him.

If anyone doubts that competitiveness—not alcohol—makes the alcoholic, he should attend meetings of Alcoholics

Anonymous and listen to the boasting that goes on among members. Each insists he has been, in his day, the worst drunk of the lot. It is such open and flagrant exaggeration most of the time that they even laugh at each other's tall tales. No one will agree that the other fellow was a bigger drunk than he was in his time.

If an alcoholic manages to stay dry for several months, he begins to get a swelled head over that too. It becomes the basis for more bragging and for a moralistic attitude toward anyone who may have slipped. The other members of the group can't stand such competition, of course, so they have to take this character down a peg. They let him know in an unmistakable way that he is suffering from "halo pressure" and that he had better shrink his head a bit because they're getting tired of him.

The more one comes to know alcoholics as a group, the more evident it is that each one wants to be the favored child. We found that an alcoholic sees all situations in terms of being above or below someone else. No one can get his feelings hurt any more quickly than he. When his feelings get hurt, he pours alcohol on them. This anesthetic calms the pain until he can get back a bit of self-esteem. As far as we're concerned the whole vicious circle starts with this exaggerated tendency toward jealous comparisons. If this extravagant ambition to be topmost isn't achieved, the alcoholic becomes tense and feels humiliated and downgraded. This drives him to seek escape. Liquor, in large or small doses, serves to slow one down. While a person is slowed down he is also falling behind in the race to be the preferred one in the community in which he lives. So when the effects of the anesthetic wear off, the alcoholic finds himself far behind the others. Once more his jealousy is aroused, and this spurs him to fight to regain his lost place.

Unfortunately, each time he starts to improve his situation with honest effort, it is not long before his feelings get hurt all over again. He gets what is known among alcoholics as the "dry jitters." The quickest relief for this, in his experience, is another drink. Just one drink, he hopes. But it usually takes two. Every alcoholic knows only too sadly that one drink and one drink don't make two. They have learned that one and one make eleven! So there he is again, in the middle of his next binge. He repeats this process again and again. Growing discouragement pushes him around the vicious circle faster and faster.

It became our conclusion, therefore, that there is rarely any lasting improvement until the alcoholic learns that this is central to his difficulty and gives up his habit of jealous competition. We have been told by those who keep statistics that the incidence of alcoholism begins to thin out in the age range beyond fifty or sixty. We have been led to wonder if this happens because the struggle to be on top becomes of less importance to any person in the latter part of life. Isn't it logical to assume that the need for alcohol may recede as the need to compare oneself or to compete against others recedes? And this factor may account for those reforms that take place before a ripe age is reached.

We are not saying that everyone caught in the habit of jealous competition turns into an alcoholic, but that every alcoholic is seriously handicapped by this tendency. He can't keep his own show on the road. We still do not know why some people express their jealousy by alcoholic binges whereas others use overeating, sexual athletics, drug addiction, invalidism, and similar avenues of escape from the pain of frustrated jealous competition. We may never know why one chooses one way and one another, but we feel the central core of all kinds of addiction is the same. All such addictions are in the nature of end results, not causes, as so many have thought.

The habit of competing in this manner starts in childhood. Once it is ingrained, a person carries it into all of his life situations, quite unaware that it is the source of his misery. This may explain why will power isn't of much help in the case of the alcoholic. He feeds himself on the poison of jealousy faster than he consumes alcohol. How can he stop drinking until he can give up the cause of his need for a drink?

Not many people see the similarity between their behavior as adults and the way they behaved when they were children. We are fond of assuming that we have outgrown childish things. More often than not we have merely substituted new forms of jealous competition for those we used when we were children. It is important that we recognize the persistence of old traits lest we become completely victimized by them.

The following is the story of Kenneth, who believed his problem was alcoholism whereas he was actually the victim of acute jealousy. In a counseling session Ken just distilled out of himself what was most persistently bothering him as if it were a cinder in his eye that cut off his vision. It was his habitual way of thought—the kind of mental furniture he had to live with daily in his thoughts. He started:

My work is falling down and I have a family to support. I live in constant fear of losing my job. My problem is alcohol. It fogs my brain. I have been drinking since I was a young man. I was scared of girls so I spent my weekends in saloons drinking. Every night I had four cocktails and several quarts of beer in the evening, before going to bed. When I was not drinking I was reading. Now I can't go out because I am tied down by my family. I could make a fine income if only I didn't drink.

The person caught in jealous competition does not enjoy the company of other people. They are a threat to him.

Everyone likes my wife. I grew up among toughs fighting all the time. I used to blush easily but eventually became a good dancer. I can't get my work done because I'm not aggressive enough. If someone gets angry at me, I get weak. I can't stand losing out on things. Until adolescence I was very bright but I have lost that now. If I run into a stronger person, I want to fight him.

Now we wonder where Ken got this idea. It sounds irrational. But we do not have to wonder long. The rationality pops out in his next statement.

I had several brothers, and they were more athletic than I. I try to keep up with my boss.

So, he was in jealous competition with his brothers. Now he has transferred the fighting attitude to his boss. He probably gives his boss a hard time just as he probably sabotaged his brothers because they could do better than he could.

I have a better education than my boss. At home I'm the boss, but outside I'm afraid someone will take a swing at me. Getting on the subway, I stand back and let others get on first. I grew up with rough kids but I wore glasses. I was the brains of the gang I ran with. I was stopped once by the leader of a rival gang and he took a swing at me. My friends came up about that time and I beat up the leader of the other gang—but I was scared. Something that bothers me is — sometimes I make a joke and it always starts a fight. My wife and I are not in the social swim. The people in our neighborhood are all more wealthy and I don't belong. All the starch went out of me at adolescence. I am too polite to get ahead.

Ken is as ambitious as he is cautious. That means he takes one step forward and one step backward, always ending up in the same place. No wonder he drinks! He can't get ahead with his work or his life in general. His jealous competition started with his brothers and embraces his boss and neighbors and probably everyone else around him. He labels his timidity as "being too polite." In truth, he would like to kill the opposition.

I was never a good team player. Though I'm on the lowest rung in my office, I'm given important work to do. It is handed to a secretary when I finish it and we do not get along. I am irritable at home with my wife. I'm concerned about my drinking and I read too much. My wife's family are lowbrows and I don't visit them. My family were quite well-to-do. I used to have buddies when I was younger. They looked up to me. Recently, I have been making a lot of mistakes in my work. I have been forgetting important things. The boss will kill me if he finds out. The secretary does not cooperate with me. I often compare my feelings with others. My wife is much more friendly than I am.

Comparisons, comparisons, comparisons! They keep Ken so busy he can't put his mind on his own affairs.

My wife is always looking out for her family. I have to contribute to them financially. I refuse to visit them and she has to go alone. There is a young fellow in our office who is smarter than I am. He often catches my mistakes but I catch his, too. He has stomach trouble and can't eat. As a boy I gave up competing in a lot of ways; I avoided physical competition because of my brothers. I became an intellectual.

He thinks he gave up competing? Well, he didn't give up jealous competition, that's for sure. He only gave up trying where he was convinced he had no chance to win. He chose to outsmart them intellectually. They could not challenge him there.

I had no kids my age to play games with and I couldn't get on my brother's team. Later on I did get good at baseball until I hurt my back. I find it hard to get up to go to work in the morning. I haven't had a vacation in several years. I ought to take some special courses in my field.

What is your guess? Will Ken take the course? And so his story went, on and on and on. But it was always on the same theme of jealous comparisons. Wouldn't you take an anesthetic if you looked at life like that? Or, would you do what Cain did? In either case, it spells living death.

For jealousy makes a man furious, and he will not spare when he takes revenge. (Proverbs, 6:34, R.S.V.)

Let us not mistake that alcohol is Ken's problem. The almost total lack of self-confidence, due to jealous comparisons, is his problem, and alcohol is only a way of hiding his constant humiliation. Only an increase of his self-confidence will help him face the world. He cannot increase his courage as long as he makes comparisons which put him at cross-purposes with those around him.

## 15

## *FOOD CAN BE A WEAPON*

Addictions are basically all alike. That is, an addiction moves in and takes over as a kind of soothing syrup when the pain of frustrating, jealous competition becomes too much. Overeating is an example. It is less dramatic than alcoholism but it is more prevalent. It is an addiction in the sense that the overeater seems to have no control over his cravings. He becomes seriously overweight, endangers his health, and hates himself for being so ungainly. Yet he fails in attempts to correct his condition.

Here is the story of a pretty woman who struggled hopelessly to regain her figure only to catch herself at the door of the refrigerator again and again. Ruth's story begins:

I love my family—but I have no satisfaction in life.

We do not believe that she loves anyone. Let us see what she does. We predict that her words are not where her feet are going. Our training prepared us to understand that a "Yes, but . . ." really means "no!" We must be prepared to hear complaints about members of her family as her story progresses. When someone tells us he has no satisfaction in life, we are reminded again of Cain, who tilled the soil endlessly with the soil not yielding its nourishment to him.

I was a very unhappy kid and hated my mother. I was always a nonconformist. I tested people out by putting on small scenes over trivial things to see how far I could go with them. I still do. I was always overweight and I have gained fifty pounds since my marriage.

The competitive person always has to set up conflicts to test the limits of his powers. Certainly, fifty pounds is a cruel test of her husband's affection. There must be kinder ways of testing him.

I am moody but my husband puts up with my moodiness. I am easily angered by how things are said to me and I get very touchy. It bothers me that we have so little money. I am really a good designer and love to make pretty things for others. I love furniture and fabrics. My mind is full of creative ideas—so full that I can't sleep nights for thinking about them. I want lovely things, and cheap materials depress me. All our friends have more money than we have.

We can always be sure that hypersensitivity means that a person is caught in jealous competition. It is with such people that we must weigh our words on a jeweler's scale lest we hurt their feelings. Of course, it would have been useless for this woman to make beautiful clothes for herself, because she couldn't wear them well with all that excess weight. But she could earn praise from others by the things she dreamed up lying awake nights. Most insomnia, if not all, comes from jealous competition. It means a person works at night as well as in the daytime on the problem of how to surpass those around him even though he may feel hopeless about doing so. Ruth has the same idea that most jealous people have—that she would be happy if only she had as much money as her friends. She feels put back at being so far behind the high goal she sets for her competition, and gets depressed.

Our furniture is not attractive and our house isn't either. So I seldom invite our friends to visit us. They are very superficial and are only interested in appearances.

The meaning of this competitive comparison is "Thank God, I am not as they are" . . . isn't it?

We can't afford to fix up the house the way it ought to be and I can't stand cheap things, so we might as well keep what we have.

Can you think of a better way to depress yourself? Why not use one's designing taste to make the best of what one has, rather than use it only to make fine things for others— especially as they are superficial?

I did not get along with my father. He favored my brother. He didn't get along with my mother. My brother and I don't get along but he used to look up to me and ask my advice.

Ruth told us earlier that she was a nonconformist. Apparently, her idea of being a nonconformist was to fight with everyone. And she still does but in more hidden ways.

My husband is a little too even-tempered with me but he gets angry when he thinks I am trying to alienate him from his family. I do not like them. I am an extremely selfish person and his mother can always get my back up. I still discuss things with my own mother but it always ends up in a fight. I've always been critical of her all my life.

Well, now, we see that no relationship at all escapes her destructive competition!

I had a fight with a relative who disagreed with my taste in design. She is very jealous of me. After the fight, I went out to the icebox and ate everything in sight.

The rest of this story does not need to be presented, for it doesn't change in content. This much is enough to show that this woman is caught in the same vicious circle as the alcoholic. First there's the jealous competition extending all the way back to childhood. It is this that gives Ruth the feeling of being put back and "empty." When she feels "empty," she seeks food even though she is not physically hungry. This produces a feeling of guilt, which makes her feel more put back than before. Then comes more emptiness. So it goes—round and round and round, the same as with the alcoholic.

Rigid dieting may take off a few pounds while such a person is at a "milk farm" where there is a competition in not eating. But a return to the previous environment and the jealous problems one has set up in the past starts the whole thing over again. Nothing other than a reduction in the jealous attitude will permit such an individual to give up compulsive eating.

We have found that undereating can also be an expression of jealous competition. As a general rule we might say that any departure from matter-of-fact behavior is suspect in our eyes. One should eat and not occupy others unduly with this function. If eating becomes a critical issue, the probability is that the individual is using it as a weapon in his fight against someone near him. A perfect example of how this can happen is to be found in the story of two adolescent sisters who lived in great rivalry with each other as to which one could be the favored one of the parents.

The older sister, Alice, was considered the "brains of the family." Her schoolwork had always been excellent, and she was studying to become a teacher. But she was not comfortable socially, especially with young men. She seemed to avoid dating and was very hard to please when it came to the boys in her life. This worried her parents, who had ambitions to marry their daughters off to up-and-coming young men. Alice appeared to enjoy their discomfort, and she did nothing to improve her situation. The more they urged her to make contacts, the more she resisted them.

The younger daughter, Carol, was just the opposite. She made no effort at all in school but did attract the most popular boys in the community. She was overconfident in this regard, and she enjoyed casting off her conquests as soon as a brighter star came in sight. She lost no opportunity to parade her superiority in this respect under the nose of her sister. This only made Alice's parents worry more about her and led them to nag her all the more to find a suitor.

We have often seen that if one child, for instance, is good in school, the one next to him in the family will neglect schoolwork energetically! At the same time, the one who is poor in school will discover some other area of competition that will throw his rival into the shade and make him look poor in comparison. The air is then made blue with odious comparison between the two of them. This was the general situation when Carol found it desirable to take another step against her sister. In her opinion, Alice was getting altogether too much attention from the parents. The opportunity to turn the tables on her sister was not long in coming.

It happened at the dinner table one night. There was a story in the newspaper about a man who had been eating when food lodged in his throat and he choked to death. From that moment on, Carol found it impossible to swallow without choking. At first it did not seem serious. But as time went on she ate less and less while the parents made more and more fuss over her not eating. Every small bite was accompanied by much fussing on their part so that she became the center of attention every mealtime. The concern about Alice's plight was forgotten entirely in the face of the emergency Carol had created.

In a few weeks her weight began to fall alarmingly. Now she had truly triumphed over her sister. Her parents were concerned with her day and night at home and had to worry about her schoolwork in the bargain. Carol had stumbled into the perfect answer to her competition with Alice.

We can see clearly how a person can accomplish sudden changes in neurotic symptoms under the pressure of jealous competition. Neurosis is undoubtedly a competitive device and exists in direct ratio to the amount of frustrated jealous striving the individual has in his character. Such an individual makes war on others so he may be rated more significant in their eyes. Needless to say, he lacks an understanding of why he behaves as he does because he's not aware of his jealous disposition and his fighting attitude to life. He hangs on to his chance discoveries as long as they serve his purpose. Anything is grist to the mill. Thus he may choose overeating, undereating, or what-have-you to accomplish his purpose, depending on which excites the most anxious comment in those around him and wins him the center of their attention. The jealous person can make the most innocent thing into an instrument for waging war.

## 16

# THE DYNAMICS OF ADDICTION

The recent spread of drug addiction means that the problem will probably get much worse before we see an improvement in the situation. It is necessary to view the over-all problem we call addiction and its relation to drugs in particular. We must see that it is the same problem regardless of where we find it or how it is expressed. Seeing is action. Unless we see clearly the coherent pattern behind all addiction, we can only stumble about in semidarkness fumbling with hit-and-miss attempts to meet the confronting problem. We must find the common denominator in these seemingly different problems. When we see that addiction to food and betting on horses, games, and other sports is no different from addiction to drugs, alcohol, or cigarettes, then we are well on our way to gaining some control of such symptomatic manifestations of the basic disease of addiction.

One of the first things requisite to our understanding is that there are no addicting substances; *there are only addicts!* To clarify this, let us consider the case of Joseph. Joe pleaded for treatment though he had no money to pay for it. He was seventeen, and had been on heroin for several years. His goal was to get on the methadone program, but there was no opening at the time. He was urgent about starting treatment because he didn't want to spend the Christmas holiday in a jail or in a juvenile detention center, having been under confinement each holiday for several years. Joe was offered free interviews and given morning appointments at eleven o'clock. He kept two appointments, but was twenty minutes late both times. Then he didn't return, nor did he bother to cancel his appointments. This response was not wholly unexpected, since, at the time of the second interview, he had asked whether he could come later in the day. His reason was that he was not accustomed to getting up until one in the afternoon! He explained that he lived with his parents who worked and no one was home to wake him. Further investigation revealed that Joe did not work at all. He went to bars at night where he sold his sexual favors to older men to get cash to support his habit.

Are we to believe from this case, and countless others of a similar nature, that the addict is a tragic victim of some implacable addicting agent that has some mystical power to enslave him relentlessly against his will? The facts of narcotic addiction, or any addiction, are quite the contrary. ADDICTION IS ACHIEVED DISABILITY! It is a purposely engineered incompetence which is stubbornly maintained by an individual as an *exemption from assuming normal responsibilities.* It is in no way due to any weakness of will, as most people have imagined in the past. On the contrary, the addict creates and holds onto his addiction in spite of efforts that others make to stop him. He clings to his addiction with the determination of an infant who has just found a razor. Outside pressures only increase his resistance. He sets up forces equal and opposite to the public pressures of family or law enforcement. Increased pressures or punishments only drive him into more devious ways of defeating outside authority. Entrenched behind his favorite addicting agent, he denies and defies all demands made upon him. He becomes as a king who can rule and exploit his environment for its goods and services by using his apparent weakness as a weapon.

Addiction grows directly out of jealous competition. It is a side-show performance conjured up when one becomes overimpressed by others who appear to be performing more brilliantly in the Main Tent of Everyday Living. The envious person endlessly compares himself with others and then puts their heads higher than his own. This makes him feel small and worthless. As Alfred Adler used to say, "Looking up all the while makes the back of the neck tired." To look up to others produces painful feelings of inferiority, inadequacy, and self-inflicted humiliation, which is the built-in pain of jealousy.

To escape such self-inflicted feelings of inferiority, the jealous person sets up some counterperformance to bolster his damaged self-esteem. Since he feels unable to be one up on the person he envies, he chooses some bizarre activity certain to draw attention from his enemy and fix it on himself. Self-sabotage accomplishes his purpose perfectly. He chooses it for dramatic effect—like beggars in India, who lie on a bed of nails to attract attention and sympathy.

Envious types sabotage themselves to extort sympathy with which they can inflate their ego. They love it when people implore them to give up their needless self-destruction and point out what a great potential they have and the great things they could accomplish, if only they would relent and turn to the useful side of life with their activity. They love to keep others praying over them with assurances and with flattery, such as telling them what heroes they could be if it were not for their unfortunate disability which they refuse to relinquish. This makes them feel valued and wanted. They discover that they get more attention for their failures than they ever got for any previous efforts!

This is the fatal secret discovered by every addict. He has discovered he can achieve a position of special privilege and power over others by the shabby expedient of self-mutilation. Why should he give up such easy victory over his imaginary competitors whom he envies? They must contribute and cooperate to win their gains. He holds his coveted position of superiority by forcing others to become occupied with his self-contrived disabilities.

No substantial progress can be made in the treatment of addiction as long as people fail to realize that addiction pays *big ego, as well as practical, dividends to the addict.* We must face the hidden dividends it pays to his ego! These are more important to him than his life. For any who doubt this, just try to stop an addict from his addiction as long as it *still pays* him to maintain his special privileges.

No addict can operate without a sad cover story which he uses to evoke sympathy for his plight—the better to exploit. To illustrate this, let us return briefly to the case of Joseph. Joe had dropped out of school and had been on drugs for several years. He insisted that he wanted, above all else, to go back to school and to get a useful job so he could be "just like others." And he wanted to spend his Christmas holiday out of detention "just like others." (Jealous comparisons.) His sad story was so convincingly narrated it could almost reduce a stone image to tears! But in dealing with someone like Joe, one must bear in mind that all addicts are accomplished liars both to themselves and to others. Even more important, one should TRUST ONLY MOVEMENT. In other words, what shall we believe—what a man does or what he says? The truth is found only if we look to see what happens in every situation at the reality level. Then we realize fully that what a man does is what he means—not what he says. In Joe's case, it is easy to see that his words and his feet were far apart and going rapidly in opposite directions. He did nothing to gain the objectives in his cover story.

Alcoholics Anonymous found out long ago that it is useless to treat an alcoholic until he has hit bottom. If a man comes to an AA meeting drunk, they throw him out! They refuse to baby-sit an infant. And if you ask an ex-addict what to do if your son is on drugs, he will tell you to throw him out! Otherwise, you subsidize his neurosis and encourage it. Why should he change when the price is right?

An addiction is a kind of ego consolation prize that an addict awards himself at the *expense of others*. Since it is at the expense of others, we must be most aware of the role the addict plays to trick us into supporting him. Parents are his easiest victims—especially mothers. The addict always claims to be a victim, which means that he will take no responsibility for his behavior. He claims to be a victim born to lose! This and his breast-beating is supposed to make him blameless, with no responsibility for what happens. And, as a victim, he is obviously free to do as he pleases, since he insists his behavior is beyond his control.

Once he has established the role of martyr, the addict uses it as fuel to feed the fire of self-pity, without which he cannot carry on and justify to himself his exploitation of those around him. Jealousy demands that he be one up on others. And if he cannot get this recognition legitimately by useful contribution to the group, he can achieve notoriety or ego inflation by self-crucifixion and thus manage to put his head higher than the crowd. His main purpose is to get personal recognition (publicity) for himself to inflate his ego. Martyrdom is guaranteed to do it. It is absolutely front-page!

This is the explanation of the simple anatomy of all addiction. It is always a copout for a person when it gets too hot in the kitchen for his tender ego. Unfortunately, the word addict has been a panic word for many years. Parents, in common parlance, "go ape" when they discover their child is using drugs. That is because there are all kinds of myths about the magical power certain drugs and substances have to enslave an individual against *his will* and hold him a helpless prisoner. This is romantic nonsense which makes excellent Dr. Fu Manchu stories and other horror stories. But *no one is enslaved from outside himself.* If a man or a country is destroyed, it is always from within. Jesus said: "... not what goes into a mouth defiles a man, but what comes out of the mouth, this defiles a man. . . . what comes out of the mouth proceeds from the heart." (Matthew 15:11, 18, R.S.V.) In other words, there are no things that have the arbitrary power to destroy; only what is within can destroy us. And Buddha, after his Enlightenment, said: "Be a Lamp unto your own feet, do not look outside yourself; there is nothing there."

Ever since Eve took the first bite of forbidden fruit in the Garden of Eden, man has been looking far and wide outside himself for things to blame so that he can escape full responsibility for his personal behavior. If he succeeds, he boasts; if he fails, he blames something outside of himself. So it is not entirely strange—considering that man has tried throughout history to find something to blame for his mistakes—that he has blamed drugs and other narcotics which ease the pain of his endless jealousies.

The so-called addicting substances have one thing in common; they are the candy, or the forbidden fruit, one eats when he feels put down by an unloving world. Almost anything can serve to help him lick his wounds when he has been thwarted in his demand for special recognition. He can use alcohol, drugs, money, sex, food, violence, gambling, psychosis, or numberless other diversions which can serve his purpose.

On close examination, one finds that alcohol and drugs have no more sinister power to enslave than innocent starch and sugar have to enslave an obese person who eats too much of them. Let us take a look at addiction by nontoxic substances, as in the case of Charlie with his candy bar jags. Charlie was the youngest of his family. He was hypnotized by the success of his oldest brother, who made a name for himself in publicity. Charlie felt neglected as a child because his parents were too busy to pay much attention to him. He did not know how to associate easily with other kids so that his feelings were easily hurt. It took very little to make him feel put back and jealous. Eating was his refuge. He became obese and then used his obesity as an excuse for not associating with his peer group.

As an adult, Charlie struggled to lose weight. For weeks he remained faithfully on restricted diets and was proud of his rapid loss of weight. Without warning, however, he would rush out and savagely devour one candy bar after another and put back on all the weight he had just lost. Shall society regard candy an addicting agent and forbid its use? What happened during the Prohibition era when alcohol was made illegal? All that happened was that many were stimulated to begin drinking who would never have thought of it before when it was legal. Drinking became the fashionable thing to do. And, worse still, we opened up a whole area for crime to bootleggers, who rushed in to supply the new customers created by prohibition. The same thing is happening now with drugs because of our approach to the problem. But this time the users are largely children who are also becoming the pushers! They get their drug supply free by selling a surplus to new customers whom they seduce by the glamour of the scene—just as the speak-easies did during the Prohibition era.

To return to Charlie and his candy bar jags. We found that he went out on his sudden binges only when he had suffered a setback to his feelings in his work, with his wife, or in his relations with his relatives, with whom he remained actively competitive. While his kite was flying high, he lost weight easily and food was not an addicting poison to him. But when he hit a rough spot and someone got ahead of him, he sabotaged himself with candy bars to kill the pain. Is this different from the one who uses drugs? In either case, the goal is the same—achieved incompetence, better known as a copout.

There is no doubt that hard drugs present serious problems, each unique to itself. Heroin is the present star in the act. And although many believe that heroin has special power to enslave and destroy, ex-addicts who had been on drugs for years state that they tried all the drugs and kicked each of them when it suited their purpose. William Burroughs, in his book *Naked Lunch,* makes this abundantly clear as his personal experience over many years. No drug is so very hard to kick since they are all rapidly eliminated by the body. In a few days no trace remains of the drug. Withdrawal of the drug sometimes is painful, but it is a transient thing. So it is obviously *not the drug which is the addicting agent.* Frightened, hysterical parents, lawmakers, and others who do not understand the facts of addiction distort the drug picture in their minds and make the drug the scapegoat. They do not see that the basic problem is Persisting Infantilism. The addict, regardless of age, wants to stay a baby and remain irresponsible.

Those who want to blame drugs choose to ignore the facts. The gambler who constantly plays the horses is one of the most difficult of addicts to help. He repeatedly puts his whole week's salary on horse races and loses it most of the time in spite of the fact that his family may not have money for the basic necessities of life. He is addicted to horse races. But no one in his right mind imagines that he got this tragic habit of gambling on horses from eating horse meat—cooked or otherwise! Gambling is a hostile activity because it is based on a jealous effort to profit by the losses of fellow addicts—an effort to get one up on another. And though there is no addicting substance to blame, the gambler's withdrawal symptoms are just as painful when he quits.

Government efforts to solve the drug problem by punitive action against drug addicts or by drying up the supply of drugs have not reduced the problem. Sending addicts to Lexington in the old days was futile, as most of them returned to their old ways after release. As for the effort to stop the sale of drugs, narcotics agents play cops-and-robbers with the pushers. On rare occasions they catch a few and bag a few pounds of drugs. Big publicity is given to such events in our mass media. As a result, many people imagine something fundamental is being done about the problem. The piddling amount of drugs confiscated is like a drop of water in the ocean, compared to the amount used in one day in this country. Its interception makes no difference at all to the basic problem. As in the prohibition of alcohol, the suppliers can always keep far ahead by working to fill the growing demand. In addition, prohibition makes the drug more exciting to many who would not be interested otherwise. The element of risk makes the drug glamorous and challenging—especially to young rebels who enjoy defying authority.

Let us take a closer look at how each new generation is recruited into the use of such substances as alcohol, nicotine, opium derivatives, barbiturates, et cetera. In the New York *Daily News* of February 27, 1970, there was a story of a twelve-year-old boy. It is a typical story of the way in which any new thing is spread when its time has come. It spreads by contact with those susceptible to imitation. The boy's name was Ralph. He was described as a skinny, sixty-pound boy about four feet tall. He was a dope addict and a pusher. He had come to testify before a legislative committee. He had had his last shot of heroin eight days before. He explained to the legislators: "Nobody taught me, nobody forced me, but I didn't want to be left out when my friends used drugs. [Jealous competition!] I started by sniffing glue and cleaning fluid, then I smoked pot, snorted heroin, skin-popped, and mainlined." None of his six older siblings used drugs. But he said, "Most of my friends use drugs now and I wanted to be one of them."

Ralph maintained a heroin habit for six months before being taken to Odyssey House for help. He said he had sold drugs to other kids around his school. The drugs were given to him by adults and bigger kids. He supported his habit at first by stealing pocketbooks and breaking into apartments. With the help of others, he mugged people sometimes. True to the code, he refused to give any details about his supplier.

If you remember your first cigarette, your first drink, or similar experiments with life, you will remember that it was one of the in things to do at that time, and, like Ralph, you wanted to be with the scene. You were jealous of your friends' grownup-ness. And it was also a way of thumbing your nose at parents, teachers, and similar authority figures because you were jealous of their adult privileges. During Prohibition, drinking bathtub gin was the in thing to do, and you had to have a flask on your hip if you wanted to rate at a dance. Today, the name of the game is the same; only the labels have changed—to pot, speed, mescaline, and other drugs.

In short, the factor that is really spreading the use of drugs is simply jealous emulation. Now we call it oneupmanship. Jealousy in modern dress! We have a gigantic educational job to do if we want to make any impression on the rising tide of drug addiction. We must kill the glamour—and the myth that indicates drugs have a mystical power in and of themselves either to enhance or to enslave a person. Then we must expose the deciding role that jealousy plays in producing envious imitation and oneupmanship with others. Most of all, we must expose the hidden arrogance at the heart of all addictions—the hidden subjective feeling of personal superiority the addict secretly nurtures over the nonaddicts he exploits. Nor should we forget the hidden fringe benefits the addict gets from those who support him in his delinquency, such as parents, who, out of their deep pride, subsidize a child's delinquency.

Strange as it may seem to many people, the addict secretly feels quite superior to those who do not indulge. He doesn't suffer from feelings of self-contempt, as some schools of psychology believe; he doesn't hate himself. The addict is an envious person who feels he has been wrongly deprived of what is due him in this world and demands compensation for his hardship. He suffers from sour grapes! He pretends to himself to have a sublime contempt for those things others have but which he doesn't have. He has to put them down to console himself. As Gary Guttierre, an ex-addict who runs Phoenix House at Hart Island, has said, "Every addict wants to be a square with a lunch box, a wife, and two kids."

Addicts are dropouts from life. Their jealousy places them at cross-purposes to others. They are lonely people as a result and seek others of their own kind for mutual comfort. They act as if they belong to some exclusive club with a restricted membership. In this club, they strengthen a common bond by boasting of their own behavior and making a common front against those who may try to cure them. They shun all squares. Out of their feeling of superiority, with its loneliness, grows a fierce urge to convert others to their club to help support their rebellion against traditional behavior.

If we are to help addicts, it is unwise to approach them in the role of God's special agent sent from above to save the damned. This can only make them disdainful and defensive. It is we who are in the weak position, for we are asking favors of them when we implore them to discontinue what they're doing and go to work. The best we have to offer them is help out of their loneliness and a path out of isolation back to participation.

We must approach them with modesty if we wish to be heard at all. Lest we forget it, at the core of addiction is a fireball of rage, defiance, frustrated willfulness, and the desire to rule, exploit, and murder. This core is surrounded by a cloud of sullen self-pity which is used to feed the addict's feud against the demands of social living.

There is an important factor that needs to be repeated until it becomes common knowledge. Since heroin and similar toxic drugs are so rapidly eliminated from the body, why does the addict return to his drug as soon as he is released from the custody of the law? Why doesn't he stay off while he is ahead? Is this the evidence that proves conclusively that such drugs do have addicting power? Obviously not. Cigarette smokers abstain for days, weeks, months, and sometimes years. If they go back to smoking, it is usually because of boredom and loneliness. Smoking is a pal for an empty hour. An alcoholic may often stop drinking for indefinite periods, but all his friends are drinkers and he feels lonely without their company. He misses his friendly crutch. He starts nipping again. In short, any addict, regardless of the thing he uses to take his trip to Fairyland, can kick the habit when and for as long as he chooses. But his return to his addiction depends on the hidden advantages he had to give up when he quit.

Let us illustrate this. Arthur was the only son of a doting widow who tied him to her with a silver cord. She frustrated all his efforts to find and keep a girl by belittling his choices as being inferior to him. He engineered a nervous breakdown to escape her bondage. Nothing worked until she began to drink heavily and stumbled around drunk all day. Arthur went back home to take care of her, which was just what she wanted. She continued to drink heavily to keep him home. He felt trapped and hopeless once more but determined to escape at any cost.

This time Arthur sought help and was advised to tell his mother he was leaving and would not return there to live as long as she drank at all. He did agree to visit her once a week for a short while if she kept out of his business but on no other basis. His mother stopped drinking and began to make friends of her own. She remained sober, since there was no gain to be had by returning to alcohol. At last, Arthur had a completely independent life for himself.

The first real breakthrough in treating addiction came when Alcoholics Anonymous did its pioneering work. Previously, efforts had been made by medicine, psychiatry, religion, law-enforcement, and other disciplines without any fundamental success in the face of the mounting problem. The astonishing success of AA encouraged other kinds of addicts to follow the same format. Each has adapted the basic approach to its special communicants and with the same kind of success. For drugs, there are Synanon, Odyssey House, Phoenix House, and other related groups that are growing rapidly in experience and numbers. In short, when addicts begin to work on their own problem without turning outside themselves for help, they begin to find the way out of the trap.

A common factor of these organizations is that they take the glamour out of addiction. They "smirch the clean escutcheon" or "spit in the soup," as Adler used to express it, thus making addiction less palatable. They belittle the superiority claims of the user. The addict can no longer use his achieved disability with a clear conscience as he did before. He can no longer give his tattered ego the hourly feedings of sympathy and self-pity he had become accustomed to doing. With the glamour taken out of his position, the addict is free of the tyranny of fashion, and he no longer needs to have the approval of his equally crippled friends. Also, the tyranny of jealous competition is ended between him and them so that he can find his way back to useful activity outside his private world of drugs.

The only one who can speak out convincingly to an addict about his addiction is another addict who has been through the "living hell" himself. That is why AA, Gamblers Anonymous, and similar self-help organizations do not depend on outside professional help. Such help has proved not to be really effective and has had to be ignored as not having any widespread value for the addicted. The effectiveness of self-help organizations lies in the fact that no one in the program is in a position to pull rank on another; no one can put his own head higher than another. Every speaker at an AA meeting begins with the same statement: "I am an alcoholic." This diminishes at once some of the jealous competition that would otherwise exist if it were a nonaddict speaking from his safe, lofty position and telling them how they should be living their lives.

What hope can there be for us to stem the spread of addiction in the face of its great and growing fashionable appeal to both adults and children? It is said the only thing the Devil cannot stand is exposure and ridicule. Perhaps that is the answer. Those who have kicked the habit are the only ones to expose it in that light and take the glamour out of it. When people everywhere understand the true nature of addiction, it will no longer be the thing to do; its romance and challenge will be gone. When it is no longer an ego trip to feel one-up about, we shall see the last of addiction with most people.

## 17

## *USING INVALIDISM TO CONTROL*

Active jealousy can be easily recognized without much training or experience. We often overlook, however, a kind of hidden jealous competition that is extraordinary in its power to disturb and sometimes destroy people or situations. That is because we may not realize that passivity can often be a most active kind of competitive attack and can win victories that guns could not achieve. Even the strongest person is defeated and engulfed by quicksand although it doesn't even strike a blow. And there are many instances in which the progress of others may be blocked by fainthearted, passive fighters. If they can't win openly, then they see that others do not profit either.

How many are there, for example, who would suspect that a mouselike individual, who is ailing all the while, may hide a high degree of jealous competition under the drab exterior of his hypochondria? Most of us have known one or more individuals of this type who complain endlessly of their ills or of being able only to "sit up and take a cup of tea." Doctors find no serious physical irregularities when they examine these patients. And so they continue to live as invalids, furious at doctors for being so incompetent as not to diagnose their ailment. Little do most people suspect that their real ailment is excessive jealousy.

Excessive jealousy of this type may harbor suicidal rather than murderous tendencies. For even though the purpose of jealousy is to get rid of the competitor, people of this type usually wouldn't dare lift their hand against another person openly. What better way out of their frustrated rage could there be than sabotaging themselves as a way of attacking the competitor? So hypochondria might be called a form of partial suicide. It is a way of killing oneself, so to speak, in the hope that the envied one will be sorry he blocked the path to glory. Hypochondria, in other words, encourages us to remain invalids so others will stop at our bedside to console us. We may not win, but it slows others down to sit at our bedside!

There is another way in which frequent and habitual poor health masks a jealous disposition. The ailing person has an alibi of feeling weak and ill if he happens to lose in a rivalry with someone. If he should win out in spite of his poor health, then this makes him a double hero. He is superior indeed to win against such odds.

Poor health is therefore a great temptation to those who want to win at any cost and do not feel they can overcome all others by a direct approach. And if they win no prize at all, they can always dream of the great victories they might have had if only they had been blessed with rugged health.

Physicians are plagued by the endless visits of such people

who have to have frequent appointments to convince themselves they are ill even if the doctor can't diagnose their
complaint. They don't want any doubt of their status as invalids. If you ask them how they feel they will gladly give you
every gory detail of their strange illness. What a stomach—
what a colon—what a heart—what a nervous system—what
an allergy!

Let us not fool ourselves. These are ill-feeling people. Jealous competition is eating out their vital organs. They know
something is wrong even if they can't label it and no physician can diagnose it for them. They are convinced they are
dying of something that gives them pain—or at least they
know they're not living. The curse of Cain is buried deep
inside them, and neither they nor any physician can diagnose
it for them. They can't rid themselves of it because they have
no realization that their problem is an excess of jealous rivalry
—a rivalry they've turned against themselves as well as others. Lacking any understanding of the real reason, they are
blocked from going forward. And so they collect physical
symptoms in the belief that these explain what is happening
to them.

For this reason, they go from one physician to another with
their unhappiness and dis-ease. A case in point comes to
mind which Dr. Alfred Adler described in a lecture. He spoke
of a hypochondriac who visited, one after another, forty different physicians, none of whom found any organic cause for
the ailment from which he imagined he suffered. Then he
arrived in the office of Dr. Adler, who listened attentively to
his lengthy recital and then said, "Well, now, I agree with
your diagnosis!" On hearing Adler agree with him, the man
immediately protested violently and began to take the opposite side of the argument saying, "How can you possibly say
I have this illness, Dr. Adler, when forty physicians have

found nothing wrong with me?" This gave Adler the opportunity to show this man how easily trapped he was in competition.

An early, protracted illness in childhood may lead a child
to fall behind in his social development so that he becomes
jealous of others when he gets back into the swim again.
Instead of working to catch up on his social skills, he remem-
bers that he was excused from struggling while he was ill.
When others get ahead of him, he gets jealous, and when he
gets jealous, he puts on the brakes so he can imitate a sick
person rather than a well person who might be expected to
be productive.

Faint heart wins fair lady in such situations. The jealous
man takes to his bed and hires a nurse to look after him. If he
can't manage to go that far, he will manage to get some
sympathetic person to come and weep with him. The story
of Job in the Old Testament is a fine example of how this
works out. He got jealous and his self-pity overcame him after
the death of his children and the loss of his fortune. He
developed boils and the dogs licked his sores and his friends
sat all day with him to sympathize (Job, 1, 2, R.S.V.). Had he
lived today, we would say that he had developed psychosomatic difficulties. In reality he had a lawsuit against God
which he could not settle. His situation did not improve until
he gave up his jealous comparisons to those around him who
had not lost their sons and fortune. When he stopped being
jealous his problem was resolved.

A more recent case of jealousy than Job's is that of Albert,
who was the youngest of three brothers. His brothers were
more successful financially than he. He had been jealous of
them all his life, believing they were favored by his parents.
He took his revenge by being sullen when others seemed to
be preferred to him. When his business began to fail, he

started to suffer poor health, but doctors could find nothing wrong. He was tired, ached all the while, and had an acid stomach. He couldn't concentrate on his work. No matter how many times he read things over, he couldn't remember the content.

Albert's poor health worsened when he lost his business and had to take work in a factory on an assembly line. He felt the men were not friendly to him so he avoided making contact. He felt superior to them but jealous because they did not seek him out and recognize that he was made of finer clay than they. He felt his job was beneath him. He resented not having his own business as his brothers did.

Albert's jealous competition for superiority ruined his home life as well as his work life. He would get angry at his wife when she didn't follow his every suggestion, especially with regard to handling the children. He often sulked with her and frequently didn't talk to her for weeks. She was friendly with the neighbors, but he held himself aloof from any social contacts with them. He always got into arguments if they went out together because he felt the people they visited were not his "kind of people."

It is easy to see how continued flight into poorer and poorer health is about all there is for Albert unless he can give up his habit of jealous competition. When a person becomes indiscriminately jealous of everyone in every situation, he *shuts himself in a box* of his own making so that he can make no progress in any direction. There are people everywhere we go, so how can we move in any direction if we are jealous of everyone? Such frustration turns our jealous hatred back on ourselves and it is expressed as self-sabotage.

We can see this factor working in the case of the woman who was a writer. Beth had come from a large family in which all the members fought each other constantly. As soon as she was old enough to earn her own living, she left home to support herself. For a number of years she managed to make a living writing and editing—and fighting those who threatened to stand in her way. Through school she had managed to be on top in her class and to win the favor of all her teachers, but she had had no time nor feeling for friendships with those around her. She had been especially competitive against the opposite sex from childhood, when she had fought her brothers with unusual determination.

Beth managed to establish herself in her work securely enough for a while so she could relax some of her competitive attitude long enough to make some friends. For a few years she was happy until she found they were all getting married and drifting away from her. Now she began to feel badly trapped. Her jealous competition against men prevented her from forming good relations with them. As she reached the middle thirties she began to realize she was facing a future as an unmarried career woman, jealous of her married friends. About this time Beth lost the good job she had, and, as a result, she lost interest in everything. For months she was unable to look for work and did nothing except sleep day and night away. She just lay there waiting for doom to overtake her.

The habit of jealous competition sets us at cross-purposes to everyone around us so that we have no feeling of belonging in the world. All our eggs end up in one basket, and if that drops we are finished. Beth, of whom we've been speaking, fought all her family as a child and then struggled with everyone to make a place for herself occupationally. She had only a few years of relatively happy life, as we have seen, before the few friends she'd made drifted off and she found herself without job, without friends, without husband or prospects.

Wrath is cruel, anger is overwhelming; but who can stand before jealousy? (Proverbs 27:4, R.S.V.)

She didn't dare try to seek a husband because of her competitive attitude toward males. She knew how to compete against them on the job and how to belittle them in social contacts, but she didn't know how to get along with them in any productive relationship such as marriage. So, out of complete discouragement, Beth tried to solve her problem by a kind of pseudo suicide—sleeping twenty-four hours around the clock. She regarded *sleep as a sickness,* which it is in such a situation. This suggests to us that perhaps all sickness is a kind of sleep—a kind of pseudo suicide!

We would not know that jealous competition is the root of such difficulties if we did not see how such individuals come back to life when they are persuaded to give up jealous competition. Beth, our sleeping woman, finally did learn to reduce her competitive attitude toward men sufficiently so that she was able to get married. She saw that until she limited her fighting, jealous attitude toward males she could not resist destroying the relationship with each one who became attracted to her; that she had spoiled each attempt they made to communicate with her by belittling or degrading them in some way. She came to realize that once she had chased them all away, there was no life ahead of her and that she had fled into illness to avoid the need to keep up her jealous competition any longer. Fortunately, nature shut down on her so she could not damage herself more drastically than she had. Sleep (a kind of invalidism in her case) kept her from suicide or homicide long enough to find a more productive approach to life than jealous competition.

Another case where faintheartedness and illness were used to get a competitive advantage is that of the girl who had as rivals an older brother and sister. Marion had been unusually competitive as a child and most hypersensitive to any criticism from anyone. She always managed, however, to keep the center of attention by some kind of distracting behavior which brought her into conflict with others. She felt her sister and her brother were far more intelligent and attractive and she would never catch up to them. She was too competitive in school to mind her own business, so she did not do as well as her intelligence would have warranted and decided not to go to college.

Marion had no desire to go to work and married early to escape a job. She had not been trained at home to keep house and she resented caring for her husband. She envied her married sister, Janet, who had a career and a baby, too. Although she wanted everything anyone else had, she could not bring herself to give up her jealousy long enough to function constructively in any situation. She developed a feeling of panic when her husband began to object to her neglect of him. She wanted to surpass everyone at everything but found herself unable to win approval even from her husband, who was threatening to leave her.

At this point, Marion began to lose all confidence in herself and developed difficulties with her heart and respiration. She could not stay alone without developing palpitations. Her physician found no organic difficulties and realized she was acting like a baby in order to evade the demands made on her by life and marriage. He noticed that her attacks always followed visits with her sister, Janet, and served to worry the sister about her health. At the same time, Marion's husband and all others had to be more lenient in their expectations while she was ill. And that was the purpose of her illness; she won the competitive advantage over the environment by producing symptoms instead of by being fruitful and productive. As she learned to give up jealous competition in favor of being more productive, the illness disappeared.

Then there was the adolescent girl who used illness to win in a competition. For a number of years Debra had an irritation of the skin on her hands and arms. Physicians diagnosed it as emotional in origin rather than from some organic cause. She was at an age where girls were dating boys, but she clung to the family although she was jealous of the girls who did have dates. She made her parents unhappy by her complaints about her skin and she wanted to talk of nothing but her own unhappiness at school and everywhere. Everyone had fastened their attention on Debra's itching hands by the time she got through dealing with them. However, although she wanted to have everything to herself, she didn't; she had a younger sister, Thelma.

Thelma was a very aggressive child who refused to be overlooked a single minute. She was constantly inventing ways to distract the attention of the parents from looking at her sister's hands. She wanted them to look at her. Debra believed that Thelma was favored by the parents and resented her interference. Between these two daughters, the parents had no peace at all because they were forever having to placate one or the other.

There was no question as to what was wrong with the itching skin. Debra really had a little sister who "got under her skin." And in a most irritating way. The jealous competition between Debra and Thelma to entrap their parents was the source of the difficulties on all sides. When the parents came to understand the jealousy of their daughters as the source of the skin condition, they taught both girls to mind their own business instead of competing against each other. As a result, Debra soon began to show an interest in going out socially instead of hanging around the parents as before. In moving toward the outside world where she belonged, she got Thelma out from under her skin. Standing independently, she didn't need to be in jealous competition with her sister and had no need to keep an irritated skin.

These are only a few instances in which a person may stumble onto one form of invalidism or another as a weapon for winning in jealous competition. There are, of course, all kinds of ways and degrees of being an invalid. The ones we have described were minor degrees of self-sabotage but they were strong enough to win their objective in each case. We must grant exemption from responsibility to those who are physically ill, but we must keep in mind that there will be a temptation to exploit this privilege by any who may want to take unfair advantage. We must, therefore, appraise with a careful eye all cases of chronic illness to see if it is truly illness or only a part of jealous competition.

In conclusion, let us say that because illness is granted special exemptions in our society, there is sometimes a strong temptation on the part of those suffering an ego defeat to use illness as a copout. Pseudo invalids of this type exaggerate and magnify any or every dysfunction of the body. They expect others to continue to grant them free food, shelter, and other goodies, as well as love. In exchange, they offer only the counterfeit coin of illness, by which they continue to win special privilege and preferment.

## 18

## *"WORTHY" COMPETITORS*
## *IN MARRIAGE*

There are many people we might refer to as "worthy" competitors of each other. We see them especially in the marriage relationship. The institution of marriage, as we have previously pointed out in this book, is the greatest test of cooperation that exists and it is, at the same time, the most sensitive of all to the ravages of jealous competition. Marital partners ought to be as free of this virus as possible so they will not habitually trip each other in a scuffle to prove which is superior. One partner should not set himself up as the judge or teacher of the other. An attempt on the part of either to do so forces the other partner to bring up a whole army of opposition equally strong. This results in a deadlock with forces equal though opposite.

We are all familiar with marriages between a saint and a devil. He drinks, loses money on the horses, cheats with other women, and even beats his wife, but he never divorces her. She condemns him for being a weakling, a cheat, and a drunkard and holds before his eyes her own dazzling virtue, but she never divorces him either. It is such individuals that we regard as "worthy" competitors. They are like old chess players. They are so evenly matched that neither can win out over the other one. In situations like this the jealous competition is so active that neither has much time or thought for other things in life. Neither can withdraw from the fight against the other because one of them hopes to win the victory and administer a final crushing humiliation on the other. Each wants to vindicate himself by degrading the other to a nonentity. The result is that both become nonentities because they waste their genius fighting each other instead of being fruitful and productive as individuals.

The children of such unions are usually destroyed and sacrificed emotionally by both parties to the competition. Each parent tries in his own way to have the child believe his cause is just and the partner is a devil in disguise. Since mothers spend more time with children than fathers do, they more often lead their children to believe they are saintly and the father is devilish. In this way they win the sympathy or loyalty of the child against the father. And in this way children are often infected with the virus of jealous competition and may come to fear marriage lest they suffer the kind of misery existing between their fighting parents.

Worthy competitors are not unlike Jack Sprat and his wife. Each of them belittled the very thing the other liked best. One liked fat and the other liked lean. So it goes in many marriages; one likes classical music and the other likes jazz; one likes cotton and the other likes silk; one likes baseball and the other likes the theater. Each compulsively opposes the other by choosing the opposite in every situation. Everything reaches a stalemate as forces become equal and opposite to each other. The result is no movement and no growth. They both spend all their time blocking each other lest one survive at a more productive level than the other. Such marital partners do indeed "lick the platter clean," because they destroy each other's creativity and productivity so that there's not much of use or value to society from such partnerships. A proper partnership should produce enough for itself and have a lot left over to give to building a better world.

The fighting of worthy competitors is certainly not restricted to the marriage partnership. It exists in business and industry, between groups and nations, and wherever individuals get tangled in competing jealously instead of each tending to his own business and being fruitful according to his own interests and abilities. Such nonproductive, mutual blocking is amazingly similar. One side always blames the other for all the trouble! Each is a master at inventing propaganda to belittle the other, each claims to be the damaged partner; neither sees how he can improve his own behavior unless the other is eliminated from the picture as a power. It is always the other one who has to be taught a lesson! And, as we've said, it makes little difference whether we are listening to children squabbling or to marriage partners or to international debates in the United Nations between world powers—jealous competition always sounds the same!

Now, let us tune in on a fight between two worthy competitors in marriage, Mr. and Mrs. C. We shall see clearly enough how each chooses his weapons against the other to the best advantage. And we shall also see that neither is interested in being productive in the relationship—and how they watch each other lest either get ahead. Their object is not to create more and make the relationship a richer one. Their goal is to see that the partner does not gain a single advantage regardless of how small it might be. Here is the story of a man and a woman married for fifteen years.

Mr. C. regards himself as the brains of the family and aspires to be his wife's teacher. He does not enjoy going out socially. As we might expect, Mrs. C. likes going out socially and has no interest in things intellectual. We can guess what her husband will demand of her and how she will retaliate. He insists that she study more, cultivate an orderly mind, learn to like classical music, and limit her social activities. She, of course, wants him to become more friendly and adapt himself to the ordinary interests and pursuits of their social group.

As the brains of the family, Mr. C. is hypercritical of everything. He is critical if his wife makes any observation that might be considered intellectual. He belittles anything she says and tells her she should learn more by enrolling in some adult education course. He switches radio and TV dials from the programs she prefers to those he thinks will improve her mind. He wants to know where she is at all times and where she goes. He regards the home as his, and "no" he doesn't want any guests in the house. He considers that his home is his castle and she should be willing for him to rule in it.

Mrs. C. wants to go out without accounting to him where she goes. She likes to stay out as late as she pleases without having to make any excuses about it. She doesn't want to improve her taste in music or read up on the intellectual subjects that interest her husband. And "yes" she does want visitors in the house, especially the unpretentious ones she can feel comfortable with. It's as much her house as his to do what she wishes in.

Such differences would be of no great moment if they were not used as justifications for making war on each other. The fighting is more important than the issues. The alibis may change from day to day in a relationship like this but not the fights. They go on forever. Mr. C. has his own key, but when he comes home at night he rings the doorbell violently. His wife retaliates by yelling through the door for him to open it himself. If he demands an early dinner Mrs. C. locks herself in her room and tells him to get his own. When she is about to watch her favorite TV program her husband switches the dial to something else and turns up the volume. She screams to him to turn it down. His only outside interest is his club, and he wants her to go with him to the club's annual event. She refuses to do any such thing.

It is not necessary to multiply instances to show how these marriage partners work to block each other's growth and development. It is easy enough to see how each lacks the independence to pursue his own way despite the complaints of the partner. Each holds the other responsible for the sterility of the relationship. Each expects the other to make all the compromises.

Worthy competitors of this sort are like litigants in a lawsuit, continuing to accuse each other while they await the decision of the judge. Unfortunately, there's no court and no judge in such instances, and the children of such marriages are often the victims. We know of one case where a girl was subjected to the quarreling of her parents throughout her childhood. Her mother led Shirley to believe her father was an intolerable oppressor, impossible to endure, and that the only reason she continued to live under his heel was for her children's sake.

Naturally Shirley resented her father bitterly. She looked forward to the day when she could go to work and support her mother so that her mother could leave this dictator of a father. Eventually, she managed to earn enough money to support herself and her mother, but when she approached her mother about the matter she received a shocked refusal. Her mother said she had no intention of leaving such a good husband. And so the life of Shirley had been embittered in growing up. As a result, she had developed such a jealous fighting attitude toward men that her own marriage relationships were affected.

When quarreling marriage partners continue to live together over a number of years, it means each has found some kind of emotional profit in the relationship. The fact that they stay together is evidence of some hidden advantage even if it can't be seen on the surface. They are what we call worthy opponents, each trying to be one up on or gain an advantage over the other, each accusing and blaming the other.

This holds true in marital relationships where there is no overt quarreling but where the game is the same—a sort of armed truce. One daughter commented, "I never heard my parents fight, but they never seemed to talk together either. My father went to his study after dinner and Mother went to her room." Silence and passivity are as much weapons of attack as is active quarreling.

Alfred Adler used to say, "Watch only movement." By this he meant that one shouldn't listen but only watch—for what people *do* is what people *mean.* This is a concept that is helpful in understanding the meaning that any human being is giving to life. It is especially helpful when applied to partnerships of worthy competitors, married or unmarried. If one ignores the words of complaint in these relationships and watches only what happens, the answer becomes apparent. They remain in the partnership because they are using each other as crutches. For as long as they remain together one may be sure neither dares to trust his own ability or test it independently. And so the blaming and the complaints, secret or open, are only a trick to cover up their lack of training in cooperation and in productivity itself. For anything a person does he has two reasons: (1) the *good* reason (which is rooted in self-justification); (2) the *real* reason. The first consists of self-imposed tricks for assigning responsibility to circumstances outside the self. In this category belong: "What would happen to my career, my children, my financial situation, my social standing if I were to divorce?" If the person faced the *real* reason honestly, he would have to give up his martyrdom. He could no longer act blameless. Therefore he must cling to his *good* reason to avoid taking full responsibility for his own life.

Marital partners who become worthy opponents carry on a lawsuit against God and each other, openly or silently, because the reality situation in marriage does not measure up to their expectations. Their unhappiness in marriage is in direct ratio to their degree of expectancy—that is, what they expected to *get* out of their marriage. There is nothing written on a marriage license that guarantees one is going to get happiness. The license only grants one the legal right to marry. Nothing else. One gets out of any situation exactly as much as he is willing to give of himself to it. Certainly happiness is not something that is handed over a counter to anyone. It cannot be bought at City Hall or in the market place. Happiness is achieved when one isn't seeking it at all, and it is not dependent on what others do. It happens only to a person who has a feeling of inner worth because he is a person who is self-sufficient, inventive, creative, and productive—a person who has a fullness of spirit. When two emotionally mature people enter marriage, they are prepared to *give* something to it and they have a chance to build a productive life together. Only in such instances does happiness follow as a concomitant.

However, if two people seek marriage as an escape from a

feeling of lack and inadequacy—an escape from personal responsibility and initiative—they will feel cheated and deprived. They will start blaming each other. The blaming is only a way of covering up their own immaturity and the emotional parsimony in their lives—to cover up the lack of courage to live fully, creatively, and productively as mature adults.

In too many instances fighting and tearing down become the aims in such marriages. They have the mark of Cain upon them. It very often happens that nothing can be done with or for the partners because any attempt to approach them may intensify their belligerence toward each other and increase their determination to prove the partner the offender. It may even result in their joining forces to defeat the effort to help them.

With such fighting types it is wiser to avoid being caught up as partisans in their squabbles. About all we can do is make ourselves aware of what these marriage partners are doing— even if we can't get them to see and admit honestly the basic cause of their difficulties. Also, we must do what we can to prevent the spread of the virus of jealous competition, not only by understanding it but by avoiding it ourselves. And we should remember that good marriages do not need any help, for, as someone has said, they are "like a good handshake: there is no upper hand."

## 19

## *LONELINESS*

By nature the human animal is gregarious and—to survive at all—must live in groups. Friendliness and the feeling of belonging ought not to be more difficult for us than they are for buffalo, birds, and other creatures that live together in groups for survival purposes. Why do human beings make the problem so difficult? There could be no other answer for the way we spoil things for ourselves in this respect than the fact that we inject jealous comparisons and competition into the business of living together.

That's the way Helen spoiled things for herself. She was condemned by her jealous comparisons and strivings to sit on the sidelines of life. And yet she was at that period in life when she should have been feeling the urge to join with her peers. She was a full-fledged adolescent. But she sat out most of her days with a sour expression, feeling lonely and friendless.

She avoided contact with boys and girls her own age in every conceivable manner because she measured them as more or less important than herself. She had, for instance, a shocking record of absenteeism on the school's attendance books. She could think up more ways of truanting than most active delinquents. She used, amongst other things, fear of tests or ridicule, fault-finding with her teachers or classmates, all of whom she called "finks," hard homework, boredom, pains in her stomach, or anything else she could dream up to evade contact with her classmates. If she did go to school she would droop around and complain of "that feeling" in her stomach until she could get excused to go to the infirmary and spend the day there by herself. The school believed she was a very sick girl and did everything they could to make things easier for her. They seriously contemplated putting her in a disability group, although the family physician could find no organic dysfunction. Never did they dream that she was just a genius in reverse gear.

At home Helen performed in an equally neurotic fashion. She was a bad sport about everything, never smiled or seemed pleased about anything, flew into a temper tantrum whenever she was thwarted, and would spend the rest of the day in torrents of tears. If she was asked to do something around the house she would contrive to do it so ineptly that she would never be asked to help again. That's one way to get out of being held responsible for any household chores. Thus did she play the role of a queen. As a result, Helen's step-mother became her lackey, doing everything for her—even to fighting her battles for her.

How could such an intelligent and attractive girl as Helen get that way? Well, when she was two or three her mother died, and her maternal grandmother was in charge of her upbringing for a time until her father remarried. During this period she was badly prepared for life. Her grandmother scared her so about other children that she became suspicious and unfriendly. She cried whenever another child came near her. She was always promptly rescued and allowed to believe the other child had meant to harm her.

When Helen's father fell in love again and remarried, her grandmother called his new wife a witch. And all the relatives on her mother's side talked against and gossiped about her stepmother. When she went to live in her father's home again, her mother's relatives put her up to reporting to them by telephone or any other means whatever happened between her father and his new wife—and especially any time she was crossed by either of them.

Is it any wonder that Helen not only distrusted her stepmother but showed her nothing except hostility? As time passed, and encouraged by her mother's relatives, she grew very jealous of her stepmother's attachment to her father. As a result she adopted many tricks to tyrannize over her father. Whenever he made plans to take his wife out, Helen could carry on hysterically to such an extent that they felt they must take her with them wherever they went. Thus did she try to drive a wedge between them. She complained that her stepmother didn't understand her and that no one else did, particularly her schoolmates. It was everyone else's fault that she was lonely.

Jealousy is written all over this brief sketch of Helen's way of relating to life. We can scarcely blame her—or any other child who is lonely and friendless—if neither parents nor schools give them proper training in the business of living together. How else can children learn that in order to have a friend one has to be a friend unless the adults in their environment give them this perspective about their fellow man?

Unfortunately, "as the twig is bent, so does the tree incline." We have found that chronic loneliness—which always stems from mistraining in childhood—is the most frequent complaint of adults with emotional difficulties. There never was a neurosis that didn't have a "well of loneliness" in the middle of it. A competitively oriented person may be surrounded by thousands of people and still feel completely alone and abandoned. The loneliness doesn't come from lack of people around to associate with. It stems from lack of training in the give and take of life and a resultant inability to feel close to others.

With such a feeling of social distance from others, we wander in circles but gain no benefit from our journey. When we are jealously competitive, as was shown in the story of Cain and Abel, there can be no feeling of belonging to a situation, group, or country. Only as we free ourselves from this tendency do we have a chance to feel at home with anyone or anything. For while we are chained to feelings of competitive jealousy, we measure everyone as either superior or inferior to ourselves. With such a measuring rod we never find equals. And when we find no equals we do indeed live as aliens in our native land—as did Helen.

If it weren't for this habit of competitive measuring and striving, friendship would be the natural state of man just as it is of animals of the same species. How many of you ever found, for instance, white poodles who discriminated against black poodles on the basis of their color or pedigrees? They might fight over a bone or some other chosen article but not about their ancestors. They have no habit of jealous *social* comparisons, so they don't make themselves as unhappy as we do.

Then, too, the males and females among animals get along, in general, much better than we do. They have a natural, unstrained relationship that is not self-conscious. On the other hand, human males and females are given to jealous competition to the extent that they often dare not trust each other. This is frequently referred to as the "war of the sexes," but it would be more rightly labeled if it were understood as jealousy. It is the rivalry to prove which is more important than the other that makes for strained, self-conscious relationships between the human sexes.

All human beings who complain of loneliness say they would dearly love to have friends if they only knew a way. They say they "try to make friends," as if it required some special skill to do so. Of course what they need to do is give up the competitive, fighting attitude they have and their unfriendly comparisons. Otherwise they are condemned by their jealousy to sit alone and watch others as they pass by.

The lonely person is ungiving of himself. He is the getting type and wants always to be the favored guest in life, never the host; he expects others to invite him to their table but he offers nothing in return. And so he has no enduring relationships; a relationship, if it is to endure, is based on mutual advantage.

When we set ourselves apart from others, they do the same with us. That is because both we and they have the same bad training in jealous competition and it is this mistaken training that must be reduced or removed if the problem of human relationships is to be solved for any of us. All of those who have been accepted as the great teachers of the human race —such as Jesus, Buddha, Gandhi—have had one thing in common, and that was their refusal to get caught up in jealous competition. They remained active, constructive, and productive in all situations. Not even to save their lives would they risk anything so self-destructive as reactivity. Gandhi taught the people of India to win their political freedom by being "independent" rather than rebelliously reactive.

Ashley Montagu, in his book *On Being Human,* claims that man's combativeness and competitiveness arise primarily from the frustration of his need to cooperate. He wrote, "Man's sense of mutuality and cooperativeness may be suppressed, but as long as man continues to exist, it can not be destroyed."

In his book *Social Interest: A Challenge to Mankind,* Alfred Adler said:

> When we speak of virtue, we mean that a person plays his part; when we speak of vice, we mean that he interferes with cooperation. I can, moreover, point out that all that constitutes a failure is so because it obstructs social feeling, whether children, neurotics or suicides are in question. In every case, it can be seen that a contribution is lacking. No isolated persons are to be found in the whole history of humanity. The evolution of humanity was only possible because mankind was a community. . . . All the problems of human life demand capacity for cooperation and preparation for it—the visible signs of social feeling. In this disposition, courage and happiness are included, and they are to be found nowhere else.

True friendship is possible only to the extent that we really feel constructive and noncompetitive. Most so-called "close" attachments are only a mask to hide a very active mutual competition. Such relationships can be anything from the average schoolgirl crush to any other association born of human jealousy. These are only pseudo friendships, which blow up with explosive violence if one participant dares to look to the right or left at someone outside. Friendships of this type are only jealous attachments between worthy competitors. Individual members of an exclusive club consider themselves as the elite or of the upper stratum. They limit their social contacts to those of the same mind—those who can "keep up." If the name of one of the members is dropped from their social register, the other members no longer dare to associate with him.

The joiner and the back-slapper are often mistaken for friendly types because they appear to be interested in association with people. More often than not, they are as much given to jealous competition as the others we have mentioned. They follow the ebb and flow of local popularity. The glad hand they extend so readily seems to be offering warmth and companionship. Usually, however, it is only the reaching out of a blank empty loneliness to clutch at straws.

Our highly competitive civilization uses such synthetic substitutes for friendliness to cover the sharp evidence of jealousy apparent in all directions. Books on personnel management, salesmanship, human relations pour from the presses. All of these deal with techniques of how to overcome resistance and influence the other fellow toward your objective—how to *appear* to have his interests at heart.

Real friendship is not self-seeking. It does not try to bind, enslave, oblige, or trap. If we haven't the jealous habit of mind it is no effort to be a friend or to have friends. All we have to do is to hold our friends in an open hand and be willing for them to develop in their own direction and at their own pace. If friendship is a stranglehold it dies quickly.

The person who is relatively noncompetitive can move in any stratum of society without embarrassment to himself or to others. He is as much at home with people of one race, creed, or color as with another. Since he does not have to make jealous comparisons, he does not set up any inner tensions for himself or others. This is the essence of friendliness. A person disposed to be friendly is no threat or danger to those around him.

Individuals who find themselves friendless or who have

difficulty making friends should look to themselves for the answer. The wallflower, the sensitive plant, the social climber, and others of this type who feel lonely and isolated have the same fault in common. Their habit of jealous competition is so strongly developed that they are eternally at cross-purposes with those around them. It is the larceny in their hearts from which they really suffer. Until they learn to be more honest, how can they "befriend" anyone? For, as we have already said, to have a friend one must be a friend.

## 20

## STEALING

Since stealing is so prevalent in both children and adults, it deserves special mention when we are discussing neurotic symptoms as competitive devices. Of course very young children steal because they have no concept of ownership, but after childhood stealing is an expression of jealous competition. This is particularly evident in kleptomania, where the person even goes so far as to steal things for which he has no need. His jealousy is so extensive that he must strike out at almost everyone.

A person steals only when he feels put back in life. And he doesn't feel this unless he is in the habit of envying those around him and making comparisons unfavorable to himself. Then he starts to pity himself to the same degree that he feels deprived. His sense of emptiness leads him to reach out for something that belongs to someone else. He steals to compensate for his feeling of impoverishment.

Some schools of psychology say the person is really only stealing love in such cases and that we must give him more love so that he will stop stealing. This would be a splendid answer if only it worked, but it doesn't. Jealousy demands everything and will not rest while anyone has anything it can use. Jealous eyes never fail to see everything of value. Very seldom do we find a person, in these days of abundance, who steals out of actual human need. Almost all thefts these days are committed by those who compete only to make a good impression on those around them to assuage their jealousy. A good example of this is the case of the shoplifter who was caught in a department store.

Sarah began by trying to hide the facts, as most shoplifters do. But when she saw it would do no good, she began to spill out her motivation. She had a daughter who was about to get married. She wanted very much to give her daughter a wedding fully as elaborate as those given by her neighbors for their daughters. She didn't have enough money for any such big event. Her jealousy of her neighbors preyed on her mind day and night. What would they say about her in the neighborhood if she gave a small, unpretentious affair? She could not endure the thought. Through the eyes of jealousy, she could see nothing else to do but steal the things she needed to make a splash. There was no other way, she felt. She could not consider allowing her neighbors to be ahead of her. She did not visualize getting caught and the shame she would bring down on her daughter or herself if that happened. Jealousy is the mother of all larceny, and Sarah had it in her heart!

When children steal we must decide in our own mind whether it is because they are too young to know better or whether they are caught in jealous competition. Some parents go into a panic when their young children are caught stealing. They have an idea it is somehow an inborn trait and that it will persist when the child gets older unless they do something drastic to prevent a recurrence. This is nonsense, of course, because a young child doesn't know the difference between what's his and what's not. We have to keep explaining until he begins to understand the difference. If he is not motivated by jealousy, it will not take long for him to understand why he must not take what does not belong to him. This can usually be accomplished by the age of three or four.

But if we encounter repeat stealing after this age, we must begin to wonder if the child is not already caught in a trap of jealousy. So it was with William, who, at eight, stole anything he could move. And it was plain to see that he was a small tornado of jealous wrath. He didn't need anything he stole. He could have had what he needed or wanted for the asking because his parents were well-to-do. They provided for their three children, William, Carl, and Tammy, all that one could expect them to—and sometimes much more.

Although the father was too busy making money to give his children much attention and the mother led an exceedingly active life, still these parents did love their children. So William, the middle child, didn't steal because he wasn't loved. As a matter of fact he was quite the favorite for a time, according to his mother. From the beginning of his life he had shown a high degree of activity and good intelligence. By the age of two he was doing things ordinarily expected of a three-year-old. He was very well coordinated and had the makings of a good athlete. In a game he was rough, tough, and noisy. He loved to play for the joy of the game, any game, win or lose.

In his preschool days it looked as if William had a good jump on getting into the main tent of life. But he got distracted by a jealousy that raged and mounted in him until all he did was wallow around in it. He had no time after that to devote to working for himself or to developing a mind of his own. The more jealous comparisons he made, unfavorable to himself, the more he swaggered and strutted and strove to be the big shot he wasn't. So over the years, in addition to stealing, he had a whole bag full of all kinds of useless, infantile, bizarre gimmicks to entice an audience into his side show.

But William was outgeneraled by his older brother, Carl, who competed strenuously to win the parents' favor. Carl discovered accidentally or otherwise that quiet behavior pleased his parents and that his little brother's more noisy activity often irritated them. So he developed noiseless hobbies that would win approval, and he worked to get good marks in school. His parents grew very proud of him and boasted about him to all and sundry. Carl sought other means to attract their attention and solidify his place in the sun. Once he amused them by parading around with a comic collection of clothes. This was greeted by appreciative laughter and approval, so he began to make a production of every small event. Then Carl took to teasing William—without being stopped—about his size or any other inadequacies. It was very evident that he worked hard at pushing William right out of the picture, and, in the long run, he succeeded.

Just as the younger boy was at the threshold of having to learn to read in school and to apply himself to academic work, a little sister came along. Tammy was curly-headed, bright-eyed, and a real living doll. In no time at all she became her parents' darling. And in no time at all she knew it. As she grew she developed into quite a mimic and comedian. She aped her mother and played to her audience for all she was worth. Again her parents reacted with appreciation and applause.

What chance was there for William after that with such strong competitors? How could he have any heart for school

or for developing his own inner gleam? There is an old saying: "If you can't lick 'em, join 'em," and William did just this.
He joined with his sister. He began hanging around Tammy.
Meanwhile he neglected to do any of the things expected of
a boy his age such as playing ball, riding a bike, making
friends, developing hobbies, joining a club. Instead, he did all
the baby things. Is there a more effective weapon for a child
who is in jealous competition with a younger one than to try
to outbaby the baby in a struggle to get attention? Anyway,
William used all the tricks in the book such as messing his
pants, making a problem of eating, and many other manifestations of infantile behavior.

As far as his parents were concerned the most objection-
able trick he had was the stealing. When William started to
steal, his mother and father were no different from any other
parents who allow themselves to get panicked instead of
looking to see what it was *in their relationship to their children* that might be causing such behavior. Parents don't like
to acknowledge the fact that a child of theirs is stealing. It's
so much easier to shut their eyes to such a revelation. Certainly, William had exposed his jealousy enough in all sorts of
ways other than stealing for any perceptive adult to recognize the cause of his acts.

If his parents could have brought themselves to admit that
the virus of jealous competition raged unabated in him and
that the disease of Persisting Infantilism, born of it, had crippled him, the problem might have been solved sooner. But
that was too much to ask. Instead, they grew angrier and
angrier about his stealing. Their panic led them to fuss and
sputter and scold and punish. Well, that's one way of getting
attention. As far as William was concerned, he figured it was
his most successful way.

At first he stole only from other children. Then he started

to take things from his brother, parents, relatives, guests of the family, neighbors, teachers—anyone. He stole whenever he felt outstripped in his bid for attention: when his parents were busy preparing a party for one of the other children, when they had guests who occupied them, when they were concerned with a sick relative, when his brother, Carl, won any special honors—in short, whenever the loving attention of his parents was directed toward another person.

And William performed the same way in school. After all, he never had had a mind to take to school with him. He had always left his attention back home on his baby sister. As a result he was behind before he got started and of course he failed in all his subjects. He was kept back and was labeled, of all things, a "slow" child. So at school as well as at home he felt held back in life and that the competitors around him were stronger and brighter and better than he. To get some kind of attention, he stole right and left.

The pity of it is that the school ever mistook this boy's Persisting Infantilism for mental retardation. It never occurred to them to link his jealous competition and his school failures. They never did see that his problem was chasing two rabbits at once, as it is the problem of so many other children. In our book *Parents on the Run* we spelled out this business. It would bear repeating at this point:

The creative urge lies within each child. It will assert itself when the child is free to shut out the clamor that goes on around him. The so-called untalented child is only a child who has been distracted into paying attention only to the rivalries around him and has not been free to listen to the voice or promptings from within himself. He is caught in a web of jealous competition.

Thereafter, his soul stuff is spent in envying anyone who does something better than he and who gets more acclaim. He watches and envies (hates). While he secretly and desperately wishes he could do and have the same, he pretends to scorn. However, he believes that the one who does something better is some kind of an authority and that puny efforts he himself might make would not win approval. He believes that even if he tried he would be laughed at and ridiculed. He does not try to train in that area because his competitive jealousy is too great and he thinks his only success in any area lies in surpassing others. Since he doesn't try, he gains no skill. So, he sits with his jealousy. His hurt feelings are uppermost in his mind. Fear of failure has stopped him in his tracks. . . .

So it was with William. There was nothing wrong with his mental capacity. Rather, it was being used the wrong way. His jealousy kept him on the run to be the center of attention, and he found the most profitable route to center stage was stealing.

All who steal are like William. They steal because they want first place in the hearts of their countrymen. Only, unlike George Washington, they don't contribute anything to win such honors but steal instead. Our jails might be emptied if it weren't for this virus of jealous competition.

In presenting the case of William we do not want to leave the impression that we believe all children who steal also fail in school or that all jealously competitive children become failures in schoolwork. That would be contrary to our experience. What we are implying is that some of the school's most baffling problems come from children crippled by Persisting Infantilism, the basis of which is their jealous competition. This we found to hold true especially for those children whom our schools today are labeling in such a wholesale manner as "emotionally blocked," "mentally retarded," or "delinquent in behavior." To us they are mainly children who use their energies the wrong way.

We know two adolescent sisters, Edith and Judith, for instance, who presented serious problems to their school. Although their performance in school had different aspects, their respective behavior had the same common denominator: they were deadlocked in jealous competition. Their difficulties, of course, stemmed from the home.

These two girls were born of kindly-disposed, well-meaning parents whose main mistake was that they pampered and catered to their daughters from the beginning. In the process they surrendered their own authority and abdicated their rights as parents early in the game. They allowed the girls to grow up in bitter rivalry, warring with each other as heirs presumptive to the throne. The girls made the home a battleground in which there was no cessation of hostilities, nor were there any peace terms. They suited their actions to their words, and each considered hers to be the law—not to be abrogated. They were so busy minding each other's business and everyone else's that there was no time for anything like learning to act their age. They used "making trouble" to extract higher and higher tribute from their parents—as if by blackmail.

How could anyone expect them not to make trouble in school too? Children aren't different people in a school building from what they are at home. Although one of these girls, Edith, bit her nails until they bled and stole everything in sight, as did William, she got excellent marks in her schoolwork. However, every report card showed her failing in conduct. She was so disruptive that she was either being demoted as punishment for the trouble she made or on probation, having to report to the principal's office each day.

Her sister, Judith, didn't steal or disrupt the school with delinquent behavior, but she failed in many of her academic subjects. So no wonder the school, confronted by these two from the same home, found them a baffling enigma. If the school had been geared to work exclusively on the problem of the girls' jealous competition and the infantilism that resulted from it until it was resolved, the sisters could have become honor students in all their school subjects and cooperative participants in their social activities at school and in the community.

Another potential difficulty for the school is the jealously competitive only child. We have mentioned previously the special position in which an only child finds himself and the false picture he is apt to have of life before he leaves his home to go to school. After all, he had been not only the apple of his parents' eyes but of relatives on both sides of the family by virtue of being the only one, at least in his immediate family. In a sense he has lived like a crown prince. All the attention, all the love have been his. He has not experienced sharing any of these things with a brother or sister. He expects it will be ever thus. Then he arrives in school only to find that he isn't even an especially privileged character, much less a prince on or off a throne. This state of affairs may be a shock and may thrust him into bitter rivalry—a struggle to recoup his sovereignty so to speak. He may set his sights on suppressing all rivals at any cost or become obnoxiously a center-of-the-stage grabber, or he may get his attention by retreating into sullen, jealous rage. In any case his mind is not likely to be on the job at hand unless he has had unusually wise parents, who have given him a good orientation in self-reliance. The school should be prepared to see his problem as stemming from the fact that he is an only child and be ready to retrain his perspectives about his importance in relation to the others in the class. Otherwise, he may fall heir to one of those fancy labels the schools are passing out in such a widespread manner these days.

With no jealousies to occupy his thoughts and feelings a child is free to pay attention to the promptings of his own inner genius and develop it. His genius grows as he uses it, and he keeps his birthright. The tragedy is that so many, like William, Edith, and Judith, are not freed to work out their individual birthright before they leave the home or school. If they were, it would give them an invaluable early start on the road to cooperation, creativity, and productivity.

## 21

## *BUILDING COOPERATION*
## *IN SCHOOLROOMS*

Our schools today are filled with children who are suffering from Persisting Infantilism rather than with those who can't learn to read or who were born with gray-flannel brains. It is not the purpose of this book to repeat the discussion in our first book, *Parents on the Run,* describing the incidence of Persisting Infantilism in our schools and the epidemic proportions it has reached. Rather, we wish now only to show how the virus of jealous competition (the infecting agent) could be eliminated in the schools, which are themselves as much infection areas as the home; and how the schools could halt the crippling effects of the disease in those children who arrive at their doors already infected.

We have had several experiences that have led us to believe that schools could do this without any additional cost and that teachers would not have to have any special training as psychiatrists. They would only have to be trained to recognize and nip in the bud the first signs of jealous competition. These signs are very easy to recognize. For example, every classroom has children who compete daily to be the leader in the line, to get to the playground or lunchroom before anyone else can, to be first to grab papers or a book about to be passed out, to be teacher's pet or the school's clown, and any number of such useless, wasteful strivings for top spot, not to mention the jealous cliques always formed by the most active pupils in a classroom to fight each other and the teacher. These are only a few of the most common evidences of mutual and group destruction, born of jealous rivalry, which take place regularly in a classroom.

We will attempt to discuss briefly only three experiences that we have had and what was accomplished by the reduction or elimination of jealous comparisons and competition in these instances.

One was a two-year experience in a mountain town in Vermont where there was one high school for freshmen and sophomore classes only. This was because it was a small, impoverished town where not many families could afford to have their children spend time getting a higher education. And, because enrollment was small, the principal was expected to serve as the sole teacher as well. Upon graduation, each student received a certificate that was acceptable by four-year high schools in surrounding communities for students whose families could afford to send them on for further education. Not many of them went on, however, for this two-year high school had a history of complete disorganization, disciplinary problems of discouraging proportions, and a bad record of dismal academic failures. All the children seemed to do during a school day was compete to see who could make the most trouble and be the worst problem. Their little game was to give the principal-teacher a hard time. The one who thought up the most mischief won high score in the esteem of his fellow students. Their idea of great achievement was to unscrew their desks from the floor, scrape them across the room during a teaching period, and put their feet on the window ledge with their backs to the room—or similar kinds of infantile sabotage. One principal after another had had to be replaced in mid-year. Trying to give boys and girls a higher education in this town just hadn't paid off.

The challenge in this situation was to find a way to catch the imagination of these children and divert it from such childish behavior to something useful that was in keeping with their age. While they had no higher goal than to compete against the teacher or each other, how could one expect them to turn their creative energies into building something helpful to themselves or others? So the problem of first order was to tempt them with some mature, constructive goal that might excite them to useful activity.

The school had many deficiencies and discomforts which had long been a source of irritation to those who attended it. Year in and year out the students had complained about this or that, but their complaints had fallen on deaf ears. So it was suggested that instead of just complaining they list for consideration anything they thought they could do to bring about necessary changes themselves. It captured their fancy to think anyone would consider them worth asking about such things. The whole idea caught fire immediately. The first step was to institute self-government, outside of curricular matters. It was set up according to the Vermont town meeting plan, and the students were taught the appropriate procedures. Officers were elected, agendas posted, meetings called, and free and open discussions held as to how the school could be improved.

At these meetings the students made plans about how to raise money for a new drinking fountain, a better heating system, fireproof curtains for a school stage, a piano, and many other things the town elders had not seen fit to buy for them.

Entertainments were planned, rehearsed, costumed, produced, and run by the students. Such functions as plays, operettas, fiddler's contests, maple-sugaring-off parties, square dance festivals, and community suppers were held at the Town Hall. The students did the advertising, made and sold the tickets, and formed committees to keep things organized on the stage, on the dance floor, or in the dining hall whenever they put on a performance. The townspeople came to enjoy these functions tremendously and they turned out in larger numbers for high school affairs than for any other community activities.

In no time at all these students had given up competing against each other and had started working as a unit, with pride in their achievements, toward the improvement of their school, their community and themselves. They came to school early and stayed late. All the difficulties and problems that had beset this school and its student body were things of the past. They found that education could be fun, and there was more interest in going to high schools in the surrounding communities.

A similar experience in changing jealous competition into creative cooperation was accomplished in an institution for delinquent children. On the institution grounds there were administration buildings, cottages to house the children, and a school. Most of the children were nonreaders and academic failures before they were committed to this institution. They were deeply disturbed children who expressed themselves by disturbing others. They were highly irritable and easily distracted so that they were in each other's hair most of the time. In the school building bedlam reigned and the teachers had to devote almost all of their time to keeping children from hurting each other. So on a school day about all these children did in their classrooms was compete to see who could make the most noise, do the least work, and start more rumpuses than anyone else. Trying to teach anything was impossible.

The institution was predominantly populated by boys, so only one classroom and one teacher were assigned to the girls. She had to function like the teacher in any one-room country school, teaching all the subjects and all the grades. In her room there were five girls who couldn't read a word and were so academically retarded that they were relegated to a special corner in the classroom and were "ungraded." Almost no effort was made to do anything for them other than to supply them with "busy work" in the hope that they wouldn't disrupt what was going on in the other part of the classroom.

All five of these girls came from low-income families characterized by social agencies as "insecure" or "unstable," ineffectual or inconsistent in the handling of their children, and given to severe punishment, alcoholism, addiction, and so on. The age range of these girls was eleven to fifteen years. All had had records of misbehavior before being committed to this institution. These included stealing, running away from home, prostitution, and many other manifestations of infantilism. Office records indicated that only two of the girls had been psychologically tested. In these two cases their IQ's had been found to be 80 and 60 (mentally deficient). Some had physical handicaps such as poor eyesight or left-handedness.

We agreed to conduct a remedial reading experiment with these girls for eight, one-hour, once-a-week sessions to see what could be accomplished, although their teacher believed that they were completely unteachable. As we have already mentioned, we have found every delinquent child hopelessly trapped in a web of jealous competition, envy, and hate. So we knew in this case that the trap had to be sprung at the start before these five girls would be able to put their minds on a printed page.

Therefore, some preliminary explanations were made to the girls before any reading was started. They were told in essence: (1) that reading was a trick and that anyone could find the trick of reading if he wanted to spend the time and effort; (2) that all nonreaders were only emotional—not mental—cripples who wanted to remain babies, use others as crutches, and lean on others to do their jobs for them; (3) that no one could learn to read, of course, if he had his mind on what others were doing or in any way diverted his own energies to something other than the job at hand; (4) that throughout our experiment the job at hand (learning to read) would be the *boss* and no time was to be wasted on competition as to who was the prettiest or who had the curliest hair, the slimmest legs, the cutest dress, the most jewelry, the brightest lipstick, or any other such unimportant detail; and (5) that attention would be paid exclusively to whether each one of them was *trying*—that that was all they had to do: *try* —and that was the only thing that would be rated.

When reading started all five girls were seated in a semicircle and were supplied with copies of the same book—a humorous book about how some farm animals learned to live, play, and work together cooperatively. Before they started to read in rotation the group was told that no one would be allowed to fail when it came to her turn to read because all unknown or difficult words would be supplied. This was very important for two reasons. First, the faculty considered these girls stupid, so the girls considered themselves stupid. They expected to fail at anything they tried. Secondly, it was obvious from the way these children lived together in this institution that they were ashamed to try because they had a reputation for jeering at anyone who did try and stumbled. So a new complexion had to be put on this business of making mistakes by telling them that no one would be allowed to jeer—that a mistake was only a friendly invitation to try again. We also pointed out that when anyone jeered at another's mistake it only meant he was jealous and afraid to have anyone succeed—that only those who competed jealously thought of a mistake as a fall from honor or a loss of face.

So the reading session began. Following the first session, the girls' regular teacher, who was hidden out of sight but within hearing distance, said, "I simply cannot believe my ears, and in order to convince myself that these girls all read as they did today, next week I must watch too."

Each girl was asked what she would like to read—if she could read. They listed such things as stories about turtles, insects, and bringing up babies and love stories. Material of this type was searched out and supplied for reading during the week between sessions. Volunteers who had some knowledge of reading were collected from among the girls in the cottage to help the project along. We also enlisted the help of some volunteers outside the institution who devoted some time several evenings a week to reading with these five girls. Each volunteer was supplied with an outline of instructions on the basic purpose of the project and the suggested approach.

By the third session one of the older girls had found the trick of reading. From that day on, according to her teacher, she read anything she could lay hand to, including recipes, dressmaking patterns, and telephone directories. By the time the experiment was two-thirds over, she was able to take her rightful place with her grade and age group in the classroom. She was an encouragement to the other four girls and served as an assistant throughout the rest of the project.

By the eighth session each girl had found the trick of reading, and, as a result, their teacher reported that their classroom behavior had come to be of a much more helpful nature. She said this was particularly true of the oldest girl in the group—the one with the IQ of 60, labeled "mentally deficient." Previously she had been a raucous, disruptive factor in the classroom, but now she occupied herself quietly in a corner with some book whenever there was no other classroom task.

Finally we would like to discuss a six-year project which we conducted in a large experimental school in New York City.* It was launched by the chance remark of a sixth-grade girl when she was told that her group was a pleasurable one to work with. She looked both surprised and chagrined. "But we've always been considered a problem group since first grade," she objected.

This sixth-grader's chance remark laid bare the whole shabby secret of the group. Actually this group had been riddled with jealous, competitive, troublemaking children from first grade up to sixth grade. Throughout their school career the members of this group had obviously been operating on the assumption that there was something distinguished about their ability to make trouble for a teacher and

*See Appendix: The World of a Child, p. 180.

for the school, as if making trouble conferred status. Separately, most of the students in this class were intelligent and well behaved. However, when they came together in the classroom their collective behavior was far more infantile than their individual behavior outside the group.

Obviously it would be necessary to substitute some more worthwhile goal for the empty boasting around which this class was unified. Every manifestation of their group behavior was as if they shouted aloud, "We are babies who must have a baby sitter to guide us *against our will.* Our popularity or Hooper rating and our fun depend on the amount of disruption or static we can broadcast on the air."

The job for us was twofold: (1) to upset the infantile orientation of the group and (2) at the same time to present to their imagination a picture of what mature behavior would be for a group of their age.

Somehow the "monkey see, monkey do" of their infantile behavior had to be portrayed as well as the fact that they must be lacking in ideas of their own if the best they could do was to ape each other's childish ways all day long. Then, too, a contrast had to be made between what they had been doing and what children of their own age could do when they thought and acted for themselves instead of imitating and following each other. As in the Vermont experience, it was necessary first to get them talking about what they could be doing if they dared to act their age independently.

So they were given a yardstick for measuring behavior as mature and socially useful or infantile and socially useless. And two explanations were made: (1) that a person who makes trouble for others is not grown up; (2) mature behavior can be recognized by whether it is mutually helpful to all in any group and whether it makes the group more fun for all.

This was expanded in several ways. One was to present the

idea for their consideration that everyone has *three,* instead of two, ages. The two ages they recognized were the calendar age and the intelligence age, but they hadn't come to realize that there is a third age which is of far greater importance. This is the self-reliance age, sometimes called the "acting age" or "behavior age" or "emotional age." In short, one could be eleven years old on the calendar and quite advanced intellectually, but if he had a self-reliance age of an infant or young child he behaved like a cripple. It was as if one leg were shorter than the other, resulting in a serious limp that demanded a parent or a teacher to serve as a crutch on which to lean.

Group discussions were instituted on the problems of living together. These discussions were based on mutual profit or fair play for all. Through the discussions it became apparent to the members of this class and subsequent classes over a six-year period that infantile behavior made unfair demands on the teacher and created turmoil for all in the group. They saw, in effect, that the more infantile children in the group stole the teacher's time from the class as a whole and that the disruption caused by such behavior led all of them into disturbing tensions and into being losers. A scuffle, for example, as to who should be first in line would result in all of them being held back from wherever they were scheduled to go. All were affected by the activities of the few. The infantile, they soon realized, were acting as specially privileged characters who stole the rights of others.

The result of such insight was that the members of this group, and all other groups with whom the experiment was conducted, would begin to frown instead of smiling if someone started to act seriously below what might be expected of one his age. Such behavior was quickly recognized as a lack of self-reliance and a public admission of infantilism and weakness instead of an example of cleverness and imagination as it had been before.

No one enjoys being exposed as either weak or infantile in an area where it would be just as easy for him to be strong and competent once he understands the rules of the game. So it did not take long for a group to begin to "tuck in their shirttails," so to speak. It usually required from the beginning of school until early December for a class to take up the goal of self-reliant behavior.

By the simple expedient of shifting the guiding image of a class from an ideal of Persisting Infantilism to one of self-reliance, each child became free to work in his own garden instead of minding others' business as before. The tragedy of the traditional competitive system of evaluation is that not every child can be the head of the class. But with the goal of self-reliance each child can achieve this necessary distinction and win the same prize as all the others because every child can learn to be self-reliant if he understands. No one needs to fail or fall behind another in this respect, regardless of whether he is fast or slow in doing academic work. When status in a class is hitched to this goal rather than academic prowess, each can feel himself the equal of all others as he learns to stand independently as a person, regardless of his marks.

We found that one of the happy surprises of making self-reliance the target of a group was that children lost their fear of being slow in learning; and as fast as their fear disappeared they learned much more and with greater speed. During the six years of this project, although some children had serious academic problems when they entered the group, many were awakened to deep interest in a specific subject during the year and sometimes gained as much as three years' progress in six months, as rated by achievement tests. In the course of this experiment the class did two years' work in one year when a previous teacher had failed them because of her inexperience.

One of the most rewarding results of making self-reliance the target of a group is that, after a few months of orientation, the members take charge of their own discipline and demand none of a teacher's time to resolve interpersonal conflicts. They learn to mind their own business so completely that they enjoy school. We found that children often arrived an hour early by choice and resented weekends and vacations that interrupted the fun they had together. Another pleasing dividend came from the comments of parents. Many reported a reduction in sibling rivalry at home and an end to bed-wetting and other infantile manifestations. One student commented to her mother that she had read and heard much about democracy but she had never experienced it before.

Troublesome children from other classrooms, where they could not be managed, were often transferred to our group. Although they had not been in on the original indoctrination, the members of the group quickly initiated the newcomers into the customs of the class. Instead of disrupting the group, as they had been doing in the other classroom, they rose to its level. Children are like adults who may chatter and gossip at bridge but remain quiet in church because that is the tradition of the group. In other words, a group oriented toward noncompetitive, self-reliant behavior will bring new members into line with it.

The three experiences we have described in this chapter show what happens when human relationships are channeled away from jealous competition in a classroom. In all three, interpersonal rivalries were resolved and energies were released to be devoted to more productive pursuits. The application of this technique in a "captive" group, such as exists in a classroom, gives a child a chance to develop a feeling of his own personal identity and relieves him of the necessity for competing in disruptive or nonproductive directions. It is a formula for "turning a child's head" away from paths that might eventually lead to school failure, neurosis, addiction, delinquency, and crime.

## 22

## *JEALOUS COMPETITION ON THE JOB*

There are many other "captive groups" in which human relationships may easily be structured away from jealous competition such as they exist in business and industry. This book is not the place for a full forum on the effects of this virus in work situations. The most we can do is indicate how it operates to cripple production in business and industry just as it does elsewhere. As we have said, jealous competition may assume a variety of forms that depend on where people happen to be at the time. We have seen how it may be expressed in the bosom of the family, in marriage, in friendships, and in the classroom. On the job it is expressed in terms of disturbance of work functions. It lies behind a variety of masks all the way from indifference, forgetfulness, and negligence to serious sabotage, accidents, and strikes. The curse of Cain is that there is no profit in any labor that is undertaken in

165

jealous rivalry, and it is very easy to see how true this is where jobs are concerned.

Production in a work unit is the result of good teamwork. Any good teamwork is possible only when there is a minimum of jealous competition active in the work situation. The whole problem of personnel recruiting and management boils down to selecting personnel who are relatively free of infantile competitiveness and then treating them as adults on the job. If supervisors are not infected with the same infantile virus and the personnel have been chosen with relatively good judgment, then good teamwork should result.

If the climate of the work unit is against jealousy, then the individuals of the group relax and become artist-workmen. A strong supervisor is one who will crack down on all signs of jealous competition. His workers know they can trust him to see that no one takes advantage of the other; they do not have to watch each other defensively. Their attention is free to develop positive relationships and interests on the job.

The old adage says, "Many patient sheep can lie down in one pen." This is the same as saying that noncompetitive individuals can work side by side and create no difficulties for each other or for themselves. But heaven help the whole lot of them if there is one vain, ambitious, restless sheep in the pen. He begins to trample on those next to him and this stirs up the whole number to offensive-defensive action. When it happens in an office, that is the end of work!

Gremlins begin to spread havoc all along the line whenever jealous competition comes into the picture as a dominating factor. Managers and other supervisory personnel have been baffled in the past searching for these gremlins in the hope of routing them to restore lost production. But it never helps to find only one gremlin, because another one is bound to pop up somewhere else in the organization. Treatment gets nowhere in the end unless the jealous competition that disrupts the teamwork in the situation is rooted out.

A perfect example of the disastrous effects of jealous competition in a factory is revealed in the story of what happened in a plant that made things of plastic during World War II. Before war broke out, this company had been making art objects of clear plastic. No great amount of technical skill had to go into the work. Good relations existed generally among all the personnel. When war came, the government allotted this company some radar parts to produce. This special assignment had to be done with much precision, and no one in the company had been trained to do precision work. Plastics had not been handled that way before. Machinists had to be hired, and they eventually found a way to do the job for this company. They became known as "the precision men" and also became the heroes of the day. Everyone was proud of them. They were put in supervisory capacities to train other men in precision work. Everything went well for a few months. Finally a snake appeared in Eden! Government inspectors began rejecting shipments because the plastic parts were not shined properly by the buffers.

The company had never had trouble with buffing in all the years it had been in business. Now, suddenly, they could not get anyone to do a proper job on buffing. The matter became critical because the owners began losing all their profit on the government contract. Something had to be done.

The buffers had never complained of their work in the old days, but now they found all manner of fault with the buffing room. They called it Siberia. They complained of the temperature of the water on the buffing wheels. An expensive heater was bought for them. Each time such a gremlin was removed, the buffers found something else to complain about. Everyone in the buffing room began to ask to be transferred to do precision work. Their morale grew poorer each day.

The management got new personnel for the department. In the past, two weeks' training had been all that was needed to train a buffer. The new men learned just as fast and just as well as the old staff had, but something new always happened. A short while after they would begin doing first-class buffing, some strange blight would hit them. Then their skill would rapidly decline until their work was as substandard as the others before them. The management grew desperate because nothing seemed to help. They decided to seek consultation help, and we trained them to look for jealous competition as the source of the crippling blight that kept hitting their workers. It did not take long to track down the killer as soon as they knew what to look for.

Looking backward, they saw that they had brought a Trojan Horse inside their walls and that their trouble came out of it. The precision men had been heroes in the beginning, but they rapidly had begun to play the role of big shots. To make their own job seem even greater in importance, they had taken to belittling some of the other functions in the factory. Having been placed in supervisory jobs, they boasted of precision work and broadcast that "any moron can be a buffer." This idea came to be talked about in all departments. It ended up with a buffer growing ashamed of himself— having to work in Siberia!

Once this "big me, little you" habit of jealous comparison got entrenched, the situation kept going from bad to worse. To stop it, we had to call a conference of the supervisors to show them that they were at the bottom of the difficulties that had been plaguing them. They were immediately offended. They shrilled, "Do you mean to say that buffers are just as important as we are on the job? It took us years to learn to do precision work but it only takes two weeks to learn to be a buffer. How can you say we are not more important than they are?"

It was necessary to point out that the government inspectors evidently believed that buffing was just as vital to the finished product as precision machining, since they rejected any part that was defective on either score. And they were told, "That makes the work the buffers do just as important as what you do. If one fails then you both go down together —the whole company fails on its contract. It is true what you say. It took you longer to learn your skill, but you get higher pay for doing it than the buffer gets. Your extra training is rewarded in every pay envelope you receive. The buffer has no cause to be jealous of you nor do you have any cause to be jealous of him. All of you are equally important to the finished product—and all of you are paid equally well, according to your skill."

After some more discussion, the supervisors were able to see that they had started the jealous competition themselves with their boasting. They were shocked by this realization. As a result, it didn't take them long to build up a different attitude toward buffers. They saw clearly how impossible it was for them to succeed if the buffers failed. And so, proper mutual respect was restored in a matter of a few weeks. All the gremlins marched out of the buffing room in single file.

The above story shows how the infantile boasting of the supervisors contaminated their workers with the virus of jealous competition. Workers, of course, are not above making trouble for each other even if their supervisors are angels with healing in their wings! Almost anything can be turned into something to compete about. If a group has been in the habit of arriving on time for work, it usually continues to do so unless someone diverts it. If a new worker has the habit of coming to work late, then it doesn't take long before other workers begin to compete with him. If he arrives on the job ten minutes late, they all begin to be just as late. By the time they have caught up to his ten-minute tardiness, he has moved on to new records of fifteen and twenty minutes' arrival late. If a supervisor does not stop the jealous competition to see which can be later than whom, there is no way to know where it will end.

We have seen many work situations in which the supervisor had abdicated his responsibility and allowed the workers to do pretty much as they wished to do. These were always unhappy situations, and the workers bickered with each other about everything. Tardiness would be only one of the ways in which they fell into jealous competition. Each would become afraid to do a day's work, terrified that another worker would do less work but get paid the same amount for the day. When any such unhappy game is played, there is a slowdown in all respects. Such things are manifestations of passive sabotage that arise from jealousy. It is commonly called low morale. We are accustomed to see it appear as absenteeism, accident-proneness, malingering, carelessness, high turnover, and excessive spoilage and in many other destructive ways. Various gremlins of this sort have been the object of pursuit and treatment for a long while with poor results because they are not recognized as *only the symptoms* of the disease caused by jealousy.

Fear of failure is a very common difficulty we all experience to some degree. We know how often this leads us to fail, because when we are afraid we pull our punches. It sets up severe tensions in the body, and these often lead to psychosomatic complaints such as ulcers, colitis, and other such illnesses. Although we are familiar with the fear of failure, we seldom realize that it too is most times a symptom of jealous competition. Fear of failure is usually associated with a strong desire to make a big impression on those around us—and the desire to make a big impression is nothing but jealous competition!

The worker who is too much interested in making a good impression on the boss is not the best worker because his attention is diverted to apple-polishing instead of being devoted to production on and interest in the job. He jealously watches his boss for favors and dares not take his eyes off other workers around him lest they steal a march on him to win the boss's favor. If someone else does well and wins any recognition, such a worker becomes depressed and makes uncomplimentary remarks about the person who has achieved the recognition. Or he may go further and do something to hamper that person's production in the future.

Fear of failure is really fear of not beating out all others in jealous competition. The more stress placed on winning, the less chance there is of a worker's keeping up to his own best performance. The effect of this has been noted in industry but without supervisors understanding why it happens. Let us take as an example a plant that makes electric switches and employs women to assemble them. They hire unskilled women and train them on the job. These women learn very rapidly to increase the speed of assembly up to a certain point. Then, many of them find it impossible to break through this barrier to get up to a speed which the management expects of a competent operator. Many drop out because of discouragement and quit the job about this time. This represents a loss of training time and money to the firm. What happens in such situations?

We can identify with these women. In the beginning, they do not expect anything of themselves in the way of skill or speed so their mind is free to pay attention to what they do. They gain skill rapidly until they get to a point where they begin to compare their speed with that of those around them. Now their attention is being diverted into jealous comparisons and is taken away from the job in front of them. They are so eager to make a good impression on the boss that they begin to make mistakes and their hands begin to go slower than before. This frightens them, of course, so they pay still greater attention to making a good impression instead of making an electric switch.

In time, this becomes a bogey which they can't break through and can't understand. Weeks pass and they can't get their speed up to what is finally expected on the job. At this point, they either quit or are dismissed as having failed to qualify. This makes them more fearful of failure on the next job and less confident in their skill. The evil result of this shows up on the next job they get. They start in working more slowly and more cautiously—more competitively—and are more inclined to fail earlier in the game. A good supervisor may understand this and reduce their desire to impress him in the beginning—at least until they can get their mind back on their hands again.

Jealous competition and the fear of failure which it breeds in a person may cause him to lose out on what might otherwise be certain success. Many people cannot pass a test even in a subject they know perfectly. The fact they are being tested diverts their attention away from what they know and into anger against testers. They don't answer the most familiar questions under such circumstances, as we can see from the following story of a store-room clerk.

During World War II, the government found difficulty hiring competent personnel for many jobs. One agency needed a clerk to maintain stockroom materials and to issue paper and other supplies on demand. The Civil Service test for this job was simple enough for a person who had had some experience in the field. The chief of personnel in the agency found a man he had known from his work in industry along these lines. Brian was perfect for this particular job. His immediate arrival on the job was eagerly awaited. But first he had to pass the Civil Service test for the job before he could be appointed to the agency.

Brian was angered and shocked when he was told he had to pass a test. He was certain he couldn't pass a test. He was given every assurance that the test was easy for a man of his experience because it only covered things most familiar to him for many years. He took the test and failed. The chief of personnel was determined to hire him because of his known ability if only some way could be found to get him to pass the test.

Once outside the examination room, Brian remembered the answers to all the questions that he had failed to answer during the test. After some persuasion, he agreed to take the test a second time—and again he failed. In Civil Service, however, a test may be taken three different times, so he was entitled to try again. The chief of personnel attempted to calm his competitive attitude so his mind would be free to answer questions during the test, but he was unsuccessful. Brian failed a third time and could not be hired, in spite of the fact that he was known by his past experience to be superior to other applicants who had applied for the job. A less capable man for the job but one who wasn't so competitively oriented took the test, passed it, and got the job.

There is no aspect of work relationships that isn't subject to this factor of jealous competition because individuals can turn any situation into mutual opposition and a struggle for personal recognition. Job relationships between workers and the relationship of a supervisor to workers and the company itself are in constant flux depending on how much jealous competition is in the operation at any given time. Good and poor morale are directly related to this factor of Cain and Abel. The productivity of each is high and each is happy as long as each minds his own business, but it is murder when they begin to make comparisons.

## 23

# THE ANATOMY OF JEALOUSY:
# A RECAPITULATION

We have tried throughout this book to round out the form and the significance of jealous competition so that its effects may be recognized wherever they are met. There is, however, always a chance that presenting the over-all picture may tend to obscure vision on details. So we believe it is worthwhile to present an anatomical portrait of jealousy so that every detail will be as clear as possible—especially since jealous competition is the "Original Sin" mentioned in the Old Testament and since we feel that it is the root of our troubles even today. This last chapter, then, will be a summary and repetition of key ideas that are implicit in all jealous competition.

It is simple enough to define the two words of this virus, but it may not help us much to recognize the virus when we see it. The word "jealous" is defined as "deeply resentful of successful rivalry; intolerant of all but exclusive worship and love." The word "competition" is defined as "the act of trying to gain something sought by another at the same time." These words, either separately or together, give us no idea of the *living virus* in its *operational behavior:* the way it goes about to stunt or kill the creativity that is in each of us. The only way to make it really clear in a realistic manner has been to present analogies and parallels so common to all of us that each may recognize its living forms. We have portrayed it in a variety of aspects so that it will be unmistakable in the whole. We have attempted to show as many sidelights as possible on the basic structure and behavior of this virus.

To understand an illness, one must first be able to recognize good health. The individual who is in good health behaves as if he had a center of gravity inside himself so that he does not have to lean on, depend on, or ape those around him. He is self-reliant and goes about his business in a matter-of-fact way, doing first things first without waste motion or waste emotion. He accepts the disadvantages of a situation as well as its advantages and expects to work to improve any situation in which he finds himself. He wants to live and he is willing to let others live.

He values himself and his fellow men according to how fruitful he and they are in life rather than according to their race, creed, color, financial status, social prestige, or birth. He joins with all men who believe it is better to be a builder in life than a destroyer of life. He does not seek special privilege at the expense of others, nor will he support clannish aims in individuals or groups around him.

He cannot be puffed up by praise, nor can he be intimidated by disapproval as long as he knows that he is toiling on the constructive side of life. He does not believe in any kind of get-rich-quick schemes that promise to make him or his group secure without having to work to create the wealth to be enjoyed. Nor does he believe salvation can be found by following a leader into the Promised Land.

He does not seek others to blame when things go wrong, nor does he use his time inventing alibis to justify his own mistakes. He minds his own business and is more interested in learning to rule himself than he is in trying to dictate to or dominate others. We know when he is with us because he acts on the useful side of life as a help and not a burden—wherever he may be.

Jealous competition is like an illness. The sight of someone else being happy is painful to the jealous person, and it turns him away from the type of achievement we have just described above. While one is thus infected, he is condemned to be the unhappy slave of the one he envies. The power of independent motion, choice, thought, feeling, and imagination is lost when this virus hits. It is such a virulent virus that it not only cripples a person's power to think creatively but leads him to spend himself in efforts to thwart the movements and ideas of the envied rival. He loses his own mind to his rival but does not inherit his rival's mind as compensation.

Under conditions of mental health a person has his own inner authority so that he feels secure in his own esteem and judgment. He is not whipped about by the winds of gossip or opinion nor is he dependent on the opinion of others for his own direction. But the virus of jealous competition destroys an individual's inner authority. He becomes entirely at the mercy of *outside* authority and must fetch or carry according to the command given to him. He cannot avoid taking a subordinate, leaning, dependent, or subaltern attitude of submission to such outside authorities as happen to stir his envy.

Whereas the mature, healthy mind that is inner-directed has no need for father figures who promise to protect and guide him, the jealous person is in danger of becoming the obedient follower of some dictator. Hitler had to inflame the Germans with jealousy of other powers, for instance, before they were angry enough to follow him on his mad adventures. Witch burnings, lynchings, and other acts of mass violence cannot happen without the virus of jealous competition killing the inner authority of each person who is party to the crime. Until he has first destroyed himself with jealousy, an individual is not able to follow the outside authority to commit violence. Fears, tensions, and anxieties are the habitual emotions of those caught in jealous competition, and one cannot be free of such emotions while he is jealous.

Thoreau said that most people live lives of quiet desperation because they are trapped in conformity. There could be no conformity if we did not fall into jealous imitation and competition. Without it we couldn't spend our lives enviously attached and identified in conformity to someone outside ourselves.

We might also compare the plight of the jealous person with that of a country in wartime. A country at peace builds its commerce, culture, laws, religion, and such things according to an evolution of its own design and choice at its own pace. But a country that goes to war is like a person trapped in jealous competition because all its manpower and plant capacity is immediately diverted from peacetime productivity to making weapons. Culture, art, and the pleasures of life are suppressed at once in favor of making war. Suspicion and fear take the place of confidence and friendship. All creative imagination and ideas must be turned toward making attacks on the enemy.

The strength and determination of the enemy become the god we worship, and the enemy sets the whole condition of our lives as long as we remain at war. We may not divert our attention for a minute lest he steal a march on us. He becomes a complete obsession. We are not free until we have destroyed him or he has destroyed us. The condition of the jealous person is all that and more. He is like a country that has been occupied by the enemy. While only at war, a country at least has its own law, but during occupation it has nothing except complete subservience to outside authority, which has now moved into the country itself.

In an occupied country, living under the heel of the invader, there is only deterioration. And it may lose its whole identity as a country if the occupation is too long in control. In that case the people of the country may merge with those who conquered them.

The deep tragedy of jealous competition is that the jealous person's enemy does not destroy him; the jealous person destroys himself by starving out his own genius and productivity. Jealousy always destroys a person's self-confidence, initiative, and creative urge.

# APPENDIX:
# THE WORLD OF THE CHILD

At birth, the nervous system of a child is an unwritten page. But he must begin at once to do an incredible job. He must face the meaningless confusion around him, form his own reactions either for or against what is happening, and respond to its confrontations even though he has no basis for his judgments. Alfred Adler commented that the child is a remarkable observer but a poor judge of life around him. The child is in much the same situation as one who goes into a movie late. What he sees and hears will be quite meaningless until he can begin to guess what has gone before. It is not surprising if he makes wrong assumptions that mislead him; out of his mistaken assumptions, he will make errors in his responses until he knows the story better.

The child must begin to play his role as an individual against a backdrop of social and religious customs, traditions, and beliefs that have grown up over many years. Many of these may now be irrelevant, irrational, or even dangerously destructive, evaluated in terms of their present survival value to the human race. Human sacrifice is still very much with us, as in war. We are still not far from cannibalism, cutting off the hands of thieves, and holding public hangings as forms of punishment for victims of our social order. We educate children by a system of reward and punishment and do-and-don't information which they must observe as rules of behavior to survive.

As Ruth Benedict said in her book, *Patterns of Culture:*

The life history of the individual is first and foremost an accommodation to the patterns and standards traditionally handed down in his community. From the moment of his birth the customs into which he is born shape his experiences and behavior. By the time he can talk, he is the little creature of his culture, and by the time he is grown and able to take part in its activities, its habits are his habits, its beliefs are his beliefs, its impossibilities his impossibilities. Every child that is born into his group will share them with him, and no child born into one on the opposite side of the globe can ever achieve the thousandth part. There is no social problem it is more incumbent upon us to understand than this of the rôle of custom. Until we are intelligent as to its laws and varieties, the main complicating facts of human life must remain unintelligible.

The child and the emotionally immature adult have at the best a myopic view of life. Each needs a more inclusive picture that provides him with a more comprehensive understanding of the necessities that arise out of the problems of living together in a nondestructive way. Life must be live-and-let-live, else there is no life. We must show the child how the need for participation and cooperation grow out of the biological weakness of the human animal. Only then will he begin to see why the big-me-and-little-you approach that grows out of jealous competition cannot bring fulfillment.

To assist in expanding the child's view of the world and his understanding of his role as an individual in society, we outlined a number of topics that should be discussed in school groups and similar socializing institutions. These discussions were called "Building Social Awareness in Schools" and were published in the *International Journal of Individual Psychology* (vol. 3, nos. 1 and 2, 1937).

Mistakes arise from partial understanding. The best way to eliminate them is to show the coherence of the whole and thus correct partial viewpoints. Many people, unfortunately, believe there is a natural antagonism that exists between an individual and his society. We must correct this misleading concept. The discussions are designed to show that society is a natural outgrowth of the needs of each individual and an extension of himself by which he fulfills his greatest potentiality and without which he cannot survive as a whole person. The topics discussed show the internal coherence of man-in-society so that it becomes self-evident that jealous competition is the greatest threat to personal participation, pitting man against man. We can see why all destruction arises from within us as individuals or as groups, not from a hostile society outside us.

We began the discussions by showing that the child is both the strongest and the weakest member of society, by virtue of his total helplessness at birth. All society must serve him or he will die. The basic institutions of society are fashioned to provide for him until he is an adult, able to stand on his own feet. His weakness in the beginning of his life grants him infantile dominance over his parents or those who care for him and they are his willing servants, at least for a short time; he is a burden on them which they gladly bear, since they know how weak and helpless he is.

Obviously, this cannot go on for the duration of his life. They must begin, as soon as he is physically able, to train him to be free of his total dependence on them so that he can, after childhood, become an equal member of society. They must help him to understand, during this period, that he can become their friend but no longer be their master to be obeyed. They must train him to become self-sufficient. Such training must begin early in his life so that he will have both a mind and body of his own by the time he reaches physical maturity—not the body of a man and the understanding and behavior of an infant, as so often happens. He learns this by the way they live with him and not merely by what they tell him about his behavior. They must make it self-evident that his survival depends on the survival of all others in the total scheme of things—that no personal gain can come to him by exploiting others.

We cannot detail the discussions here as they are developed in the original text and will only present a brief outline of the types of topics that came under discussion. We continued the discussions by comparing man to other animals, to show his biological inferiority to them. Man is not physically well prepared for survival either at birth or subsequently. Each species of animal has been given hooves, horns, fangs, claws, or some other natural advantage for his protection. Another great advantage animals have is that young animals learn to fend for themselves in terms of weeks, months, or a few years at most, and, in so doing, are considered to have reached their maturity. Since a human being is poorly endowed by nature in terms of protective devices, it takes much longer for him to reach his maturity and care for his own needs, and, in any case, he must always live with others in society if he is to survive. Even when fully grown, man must invent all kinds of things for his protection to make up for his lack of natural endowments, such as clothes, houses, agriculture for food, and numberless other similar devices, basic for survival.

The human being has one problem unknown to other animals: he is the only one who can experience and reflect upon his relative weakness. He can create feelings of inferiority. The animal's body matures at about the same rate as its ability to cope with the problems confronting it. It is able to stalk its own food and make an independent life for itself much earlier. The human body develops much slower than does the mind. The human being can see and aspire to grasp the outside world long before he has the physical ability to cope with the situation it presents. He can reach much farther than his grasp. This is known as an inferiority situation from which jealous comparisons may be formed—the root of all unhappiness. Human beings become blocked in development if the distance between their aspirations and their competence to achieve goals becomes too widely separated; they give up in discouragement and resign themselves to envious comparisons. When that happens, self-pity leads them to self-sabotage and to giving up to save face and to console themselves for not reaching their unrealistic goals and their exaggerated aspirations. In the discussions, we called this the game of evading the big tent of life and detouring into side-show activities. In the big tent, each individual does his job independently with a minimum of help and does not disrupt others who are doing their jobs; he shares the tent with his co-workers. But those who engage in side-show activities use gimmicks or some kind of bizarre behavior because they are not prepared adequately to act independently; they use every kind of device to attract attention to themselves. That is because they are envious of performers in the main tent.

It is important to discuss achievement age (skills) and the

need to keep same abreast of expanding expectations. Otherwise, there will be jealousy which will prevent the development of further skills. A serious gap should not be allowed to develop between chronological age and doing-age or behavior age. If this happens, the individual is regarded as socially retarded since he acts in a childish manner and is handicapped in meeting the demands society puts on him for his contribution. This amounts to a humiliating confrontation which leads him to seek escapes, such as neurosis or crime, depending on his degree of activity.

The multiple needs of the individual and the many tasks of living together are too many and too complex for anyone to do without the help of others. This leads to the division of labor by which each trades his personal service for the goods or services of another. For a simple illustration, there should be discussions about some of the difficulties, for instance, involved in bringing a cup of coffee to the breakfast table. Growing, harvesting, merchandising, transportation, retailing, and other details are almost beyond enumerating. Unfortunately, they are taken for granted until one link of the chain breaks down and there is no coffee. Eyes should be opened, or awareness established, that each step is the basis of some trade, skill, occupation, or profession—each of which demands education, preparation, and cooperation.

This helps to explain why there are schools. Schools transmit the priceless technology man has accumulated over the past without which people would have to go back to living in caves and killing animals with rocks. The person who rejects school is cutting off his nose to spite his face—as well as damaging the community by being less competent than he could easily be if he had this fundamental knowledge. The child should be helped to see how unfortunate he would be without such basic knowledge that school provides him in order that he will not be tempted to drop out if he finds it difficult or unpleasant.

Next there should be discussions on the problems of living together and how best to approach them with a minimum of conflict as individuals. A distinction should be made between freedom and license—the difference between mutual advantage and exploitation. Also, a distinction must be made between the way free individuals work together and those who live in a master-slave relationship. It must be shown how best to protect and maintain one's personal rights in each relationship. In short, children should be helped to see that any community or group depends on the total contributions of its members. When one or more individuals fail in their contributions, everyone is the loser, since the total welfare has been diminished; to put it realistically, there is less soup in the pot to be shared by all. The ability and willingness to be constructive is, as the saying goes, "what separates the men from the boys." Those who resist doing their share become second-class citizens and must resort to jealous exploitation to gain their ends.

People who live together must agree upon convenient ways of doing things so that confusion can be eliminated. This is accomplished by laws and rules based on fair play. Among free individuals, these are arrived at by elections and similar common agreements. Traffic laws are an example. It would be impossible to drive a car safely unless we had consented to follow a common agreement. Traffic violators are those jealous, competitive people who want to exploit the rights of others, regardless of the danger to themselves and others. In short, the way to protect one's own rights depends on protecting the rights of others, or to protect the common welfare as one's own. And the best place to learn how to do this is at home and at school while one is growing up.

It is important to demonstrate to children what happens when a group fails to work as free, equal, contributing members and there is a breakdown of the production of goods and services necessary to survival. At such times, some active minority group of individuals takes over the passive majority and begins to run things their own way for their own benefit. They employ force to suppress any who oppose them, thus setting up a dominance-submission pattern of masters and slaves in which personal initiative and growth is denied to all. In such a case, the master cannot be free of the slave any more than the slave can become free of the master; they become mutually destructive.

In addition, a way must be provided of evaluating an individual's own personal behavior, especially when he is in doubt. Behavior can be viewed as being either on the useful or the useless (or destructive) side of life, depending on whether it advances or hinders social living. If, for example, a person drops trash and paper on the street, he diminishes the common good; if he puts such things in the litter basket, he improves the total situation. Each must decide whether he will go through life as a help or as a burden to those around him. Jealous competition is at the root of hostile, useless behavior; otherwise, one takes satisfaction and enjoyment in making contributions to the common wealth.

Last, but not least, the child arriving late on the scene, as he does, needs to understand male-female relationships so that he will not be trapped in senseless competition that often destroys cooperation between them and creates needless misery in their efforts to live together. Nature gave the female a wholly different role to play in reproduction than the one she gave the male. It is senseless to try to compare the roles as to which role is more important than the other, or which entitled to exploit and dominate. If one tries to compare them as to their social value, one is back in the Cain-versus-Abel situation, a situation in which one tries to destroy the other. Only a female can bear the young. At the present time, at least, this special function is basic to the survival of the race. The male is equally necessary to reproduction, so neither can survive without the other in a total situation. No partiality can be shown to one above the other without damaging all. If one sex dominates the other, jealousy may goad the dominated sex to rebel, and warfare may break out as a result. Both parties to such a struggle spoil their own fulfillment in the effort to conquer the partner. Any apparent gain of one who subordinates the other is a Pyrrhic victory. Each must live and let live as equal members of the human race, each with his own special endowments. All skills and abilities are of equal value in the total scheme of interdependence basic to survival.

When these discussions were originally conducted, it made a vast difference in the behavior of children in a classroom, since they now had some idea of what had been going on in the world before they were born. Nothing will put old heads on young shoulders, but it pays to furnish a synopsis of the play for those who come in after the plot has started.

# INDEX

189